# UnChosen

---

by Greg Chambers and Peter Jones

UnChosen

UnChosen

Copyright © 2016 by Gregory Ellis Chambers and Peter Coromilas Jones

All rights reserved. No part of this book may be reproduced or transmitted in any form or by any means without written permission from the author.

Cover design by Greg Chambers
Edited by Constantine Jones

ISBN-13: 978-1543295351
ISBN-10: 1543295355

Printed in USA

Greg Chambers and Peter Jones

## **Dedication**

As we labored many weeks to develop a title, concept, and a base on which to build that concept and content; nothing was happening. Many ideas and titles were passing back and forth, but nothing of substance. There was nothing that communicated our experience and feelings in a manner that would impact and attract others. We were not landing on a solid concept that would result in a medium to help others navigate their traumatic job loss experience. We were stalled.

Finally, UnChosen title and cover concept was revealed while at church. The inner drive and calling to create this material was validated with the gift of a conceptual revelation.

Our dedication is to God, without whom our lives, experiences, and ability to create this work would not be possible.

Greg Chambers and Peter Jones

## Table of Contents

UNCHOSEN .................................................................................... 10

THE SOCIAL CONTRACT .............................................................. 11

PART 1 ........................................................................................... 15

THE GOOD LIFE ............................................................................ 16

UNCHOSEN .................................................................................... 22

WHAT THE HELL DO I DO NOW? ................................................ 30

TRAUMA ........................................................................................ 42

PART 2 ........................................................................................... 49

WHO AM I ANYWAY? .................................................................... 50

WHAT AM I WORTH? .................................................................... 57

AM I RELEVANT AND MARKETABLE? ........................................ 65

FAMILY, FRIENDS, AND GHOSTS ................................................ 72

HOW DO I TALK TO PEOPLE? ..................................................... 82

HOW DO I TELL MY STORY? ....................................................... 89

THIS HELL WE CALL JOB SEARCH ............................................ 95

PART 3 ......................................................................................... 116

**HEALING AND BECOMING WHOLE AGAIN ................................ 117**

**CHOSEN AGAIN ............................................................................... 138**

**EPILOGUE .......................................................................................... 145**

## Introduction

This book is the product of our experience and emotions. It is a product of the need to give back and help others through their traumatic experience by sharing our story, a story that has been experienced by hundreds of thousands of American workers. Our story is your story.

Books fill the shelves in volumes full of advice on resume writing, interviewing, and how to find a job. But none talk about the emotions and <u>trauma</u> related to job loss and extended unemployment, or the impact it has on the individual and their families. No one talks openly about the trauma experienced and what it takes to recover from it. No one really talks about how to emotionally survive in the workplace today. A workplace that is significantly different from the workplace of the past.

Both men and women are expected to be strong emotionally these days. Strong in the workplace and strong at home. Both are expected to know what to do in all situations as adults. There are unspoken standards in our society that we all must have it together emotionally. We are all expected not to break down or show weakness. We are all expected to be resilient and not let our emotions show, or let them affect performance in the workplace. The expectation or standard extends to home where we are expected to be strong for our children and our spouse. Because of these standards, the impact and emotional struggle from job loss are hidden and masked. They are hardly shared, if at all. Those that have not experienced it know nothing about it, and those that are going through it do not know and understand that what they are feeling and experiencing are real and normal.

The emotional impact of being UnChosen has gone mostly unnoticed or ignored. However, the impact is great. In their book *Well Being*, Tom Rath and Jim Harter talk about life events and the effect on a person and their recovery from major life events. In the book they indicate that, "A landmark study published in *The Economic Journal* revealed that unemployment might be the only major life event from which people do not fully recover within five years." They go on to say that the studies show "Our wellbeing actually recovers more rapidly from the death of a spouse than it does from a sustained period of unemployment."

The goal in this book is to share the reality of the traumatic experience in the lives of UnChosen people. This book is intended to let the people that have gone through, or are going through this experience know that what they are feeling or have felt and experienced is real. The pain, the feeling of shame, worthlessness, and the feeling of being alone in the world are all normal side effects of what they are going through, or have gone through. This is a message that they are not alone.

This is also a message of hope, for those that are going through this experience, and for those that one day might go through this experience. This book is for all the UnChosen: past, present, and future.

# UnChosen

[uhn choh-zuhn]

1. Removed from a group of workers and no longer a part of the organization.

2. Removed from your job in an organization and no longer a part of the workgroup family.

3. Laid off.

## - Prologue -

## The Social Contract

We spend a large percentage of our waking hours at our job and our career. In fact, it is safe to say that we spend more time with our co-workers, our work family, than we do with our own family and friends outside of work. What we do in our career, and where we do it, are a major component of how we define ourselves in life. What we do is who we are.

We as employees strive to work for a company that values us, and values what we do. We strive for a work environment where we wake up in the morning and look forward to going to work. What we really are looking for is to go to work each day and to make a contribution to the health and wealth of the company. This gives us a feeling of pride in the company and in ourselves. Providing health and wealth for the company, keeps us healthy, and provides wealth for us and our family. This symbiotic relationship has proven to be healthy for both the individual and the company. As an employee, and as an individual, we also need and desire security; this symbiotic relationship provides us with that secure feeling. It enables us to focus on our job, enjoy our home life, and not worry about basic things like food and shelter. It allows us to not worry about where our next paycheck is coming from. This unspoken and unwritten contract of loyalty between a company and the worker we call "The Social Contract."

The industrial revolution in the United States brought a need for workers; a need for dependable workers that could learn the skills needed to do their job and be there day to day to produce products in high demand. In 1914, Henry Ford developed the Five Dollar Workday during a time when the average worker was making less than $2.50 a day. He did this because he found through experience that turnover and retraining new workers was very expensive.

Post World War II America accelerated the need for skilled workers as the economy grew and the population boomed. Companies actively recruited men returning from the war, and developed incentive programs with benefits such as profit sharing and pension plans designed to keep them until retirement. They wanted to keep their workers for life. This practice spawned a new, loyal, and proud workforce in America.

That practice and feeling of loyalty has continued for at least three generations of workers since that time. It lives in a limited capacity in generations beyond those. In some industries and with some companies, the philosophy and methodology of "The Social Contract" still exists. In most others, America has seen profitability rule over loyalty, and expectations of short term employment rule over long term engagements. Company loyalty has dissipated. Disloyalty of companies and employers is driving disloyalty into employees.

Many companies have stopped offering pension plans. Profit sharing and 401(k) plans have been trimmed back or have been removed completely. Each year employee responsibility for costs of healthcare increases. Reasons for employees to have a long term financial and emotional investment in their employer are disappearing. What once was the American Dream is now withering away.

What we have seen in the corporate world is that workers have become perceived as 'liabilities' in their later years. Layoffs and RIFs (Reductions in Force) have become commonplace. This feeling, or unwritten 'contract' between companies and workers, "The Social Contract," is no longer the norm. For decades it has been at the core as a foundation for our society in America. "The Social Contract" brought stability to businesses, industries, and the economy. It has spawned growth and prosperity economically through stability in our families and their ability to make long term commitments emotionally and financially. The thirty year home mortgage has become the norm because of this feeling of security and stability. Over the decades, workers and their families have built and bought larger homes because of "The Social Contract." They have had the ability to plan their lives beyond today, next week, and next month.

"The Social Contract" has been the basis and pride of the American worker. Unfortunately, "The Social Contract" is no longer in effect at most companies, and it no longer lives in the hearts and minds of the majority of the American workers. "The Social Contract" has been cancelled.

Greg Chambers and Peter Jones

# Part 1

# Trauma

# Chapter 1

# The Good Life

Career has held a special meaning to the mainstay of America and living the American Dream. Growing up for many generations since WWII has meant growing up in a society that values the work we do, and taking pride in 'it' - whatever 'it' is. For each and every one of us, 'it' has been different in some way, whether 'it' is a skill or a trade that we discover and develop through our school years into adulthood, the result was the same: working toward finding fulfillment and pride in our work and our life.

A 'career' is an occupation undertaken for a significant period of a person's life and with opportunities for progress. For generations, "The Social Contract" has been the foundation of careers. Career minded individuals in the workforce counted on landing with a company, and retiring with that company. These individuals worked hard, gave their lives and their soul physically and emotionally to the company, and in return the company returned that loyalty.

A successful career meant stability, comfort, and a life free of worry. There was no worry over where the next paycheck was coming from. How you would be able to live, and how you would be able to retire was dependent upon your hard work which meant success in your career. The ability to plan, build a home, have a family, and live a worry free life was practically a given. President Franklin D. Roosevelt had a vision of this. In his 1941 inaugural speech he spoke of four freedoms: freedom of speech, freedom of worship, freedom from want, and freedom from fear. The manner in which companies started operating in post war America with The Social Contract delivered those last two freedoms from want and fear in the workplace.

Home, work, family, and the feeling of freedom to build and grow are all a part of the American Dream.

### Greg & Career

The first day I started work in 1991 at Coca-Cola I felt that I had landed. After what I considered a false start with another major company where I left to go back to school, I finally felt as if I was somewhere worthwhile, doing something worthwhile. After all, it was Coca-Cola - the most recognized company name in the world.

When I began with the company, the prestige of just being there was enough to raise eyebrows in conversations. Whether the CEO, the manager, production line worker, or the custodian, the name alone was all you needed. As a matter of fact, the delivery guy held the most well known and most prestigious position from the public point of view. They were the ones that had day to day contact with the customers, and were the cornerstone of the Coca-Cola image. "What route to you have?" was a common response to my "I work for Coca-Cola" statement in response to the "what do you do?" question. I felt I had arrived.

Five years in and opportunity grew as our local family owned bottler was acquired by a larger publicly owned company. The company was expanding. I was married now and building a life with my wife in our first home. Salary and benefits increased with increased responsibilities.

At Ten years into my career at Coca-Cola our third child was on the way. We were moving into a larger home on a great piece of property in a wonderful old neighborhood. It was comfortable, safe, and work and home life were wonderful and satisfying. I was challenged at my job as responsibility continued to grow and as the company was acquiring territory and growing still.

At twenty years I felt I had really arrived. I honestly had achieved a greater role and reached a level I had hardly dreamed about in childhood. As a Regional Manager I was well respected, and felt fully competent in my abilities based on the continued responsibility sent in my direction.

As years passed and my career progressed, comfort and stability set in deeper and deeper. Going into 2013, finishing year twenty-two, I was looking for next steps and wondered if that was going to entail moving to Atlanta to the Corporate office. I was a Regional IT Director and had been in the role for some time. In addition, I contributed to the welfare of the company in many other ways, stretching beyond the scope of my primary job. If ever there was a person that existed with job satisfaction, I was them. If ever there was a 'company man,' I was it.

I was extremely fortunate that I had a job that I loved doing, work that was satisfying, people that I loved working with, and a career with a company that was well respected, if not prestigious. I was a company man, through and through. I was absolutely certain at that point in my life and career, that I would complete my career there. I was certain I would retire there. They would drag my old, but happy, carcass out the front door one day; Diet Coke in one hand and certificate of happy completed career in the other.

\* \* \*

Life is complicated and challenging. Family has its own dynamics and challenges. Life has its ups and downs. Your home, your family, your church, and your job all present their own unique and unpredictable needs for your time and attention. They all produce their own flavor of stress. During the time enjoyed by generations of The Social Contract, the burden of stress presented by job and the fear of job loss was almost non-existent. The career was the one cornerstone of stability in society and the family. Landing a job with a reputable company meant security and stability. Benefits were a major enticement to new employees coming into a company. A company's goal was to entice the talented individual into the workplace and keep them. Turnover was viewed as being very expensive. The longer someone stayed in their job was perceived as beneficial. They became more valuable to the company as time went by. Seniority had a positive meaning. Seniority meant the person was seasoned in their job. They had knowledge and ability to get the job done, and done well.

Tribal knowledge of the company, the products, the

customers, and the culture were benefits of seniority that were reaped by employers. They had someone they could count on that they knew could get the job done. They also knew they had someone that was emotionally vested with pride in the company. The employee had a sense of ownership.

In the world of "The Social Contract," workers had routine and a good life. They had a solid pattern of living with clear expectations.

## Chapter 2

## UnChosen

Stability is the staple of American life and the American worker. It is the staple of a healthy and prosperous worker. It is the staple and foundation of a healthy and happy family. Stability wards off stress and unrest. Stability allows us as humans to move up through the hierarchy of needs from food and shelter to search for belonging, self-esteem, and eventually self-actualization.

Belonging is at the core of Maslow's hierarchy of needs, for us as human beings, and at the core of American society. In 1943, psychologist Abraham Maslow published an article that described the hierarchy of needs for humans. At the base of the hierarchy is physiological (food, water, shelter) and safety needs. In the middle and at the core is love and belonging. At the top after all other needs are achieved and mastered is esteem and what Maslow calls 'self-actualization.' Self-actualization is reaching one's full potential.

The sense of belonging and strong need to reach self-esteem at the next level are expected in today's society, and considered essential to a prosperous life. Belonging at work is as important, if not more important than belonging to family or to other groups. Work is where we spend day to day with our work family. The bond grows deeper and stronger the longer we are in an organization. Leaving this extended family is devastating, especially when it is not by choice.

Our work also brings us fulfillment inside, and a sense of self-worth. More than that, what we do defines us as a person. It is who we are. Separation from all these things can be shocking to us emotionally, and leave us in a traumatized mental state.

### Greg gets UnChosen

It is a Wednesday morning late in February, a day like any other. There is routine chit chat in the hallway, meetings for the day, and considerations of where the lunch stop will be. I just passed my twenty second anniversary with the company in January and routine days turn into routine weeks, which turn into routine months and years. As routine as they can be. However routine, it is a good routine. I enjoy what I do, where I do it, and the people I work with. And, I believe I am good at what I do. It is Wednesday morning, like any other, or so I thought. It is February 27th, a date that I will never forget.

My manager hits me up on instant messaging...'do I

have a minute?' Sure, I responded. My manager seldom engaged me one on one. It was usually a routine check to find out why someone did this or said that or didn't do something else. Sure, I have a minute, but I didn't realize it would be a minute that would change my life.

She called me on the phone, and although the call only lasted for a few moments the conversation is forever drifting in time and still sifting through my mind. As she read from her script I could not process the words. "As you know the company is making changes to realign with the business. The role of regional manager has been cut down to three positions. The region manager positions were filled based on several metrics. You were not selected for any of the positions and currently there is no position for you within the company."

The words hung there. Silence. My brain is trying to process what I have just heard, but can't.

"Are you there?" she asks.

"Yes, I'm here." I said. Followed by more silence.

I'm unsure about what she said from there, except that there would be more information coming, and my last day would be the end of April. She also indicated that I could take the rest of the day off if I needed to.

What I need is to be able to process this. A wife and three kids to support. Now I have no job, and I will soon be an outsider to a family and organization that I have been a part of for more than two decades. This is really all I know.

On the ride home, I have never felt so alone.

That night sleep would not, and did not come. My mind was too full of what was happening, how our lives were changing, the pressure of all my responsibilities, and the fear of the unknown path ahead. At 3am I began to cry.

\* \* \*

Webster defines 'unchosen' as 'not chosen.' That definition implies that you were left out and never chosen at all. It implies that you were never a part of the group. We have redefined the word. We regard UnChosen as someone that was originally chosen, selected for their unique skills and abilities, then removed, or UnChosen. When people are chosen they become an important part of the whole, bond with the group, and live in a symbiotic relationship with that group, team, or company. Think of being chosen for a basketball team. You have the skills and abilities and play with the team for a long period of time. You are a great defensive and offensive player. You are a top scorer for the team. One day the coach comes by and says 'you're out,' and for no reason at all. It is the same in the business world. The business world is creating UnChosen people every day. People that were chosen and bonded strongly with their direct workgroup and their company. Then that person was selected, and removed from the group, and became UnChosen. They were removed from their workgroup family. They were laid off for no apparent reason, and therefore — UnChosen.

The first feelings that come from being UnChosen is an immense feeling of separation. A great feeling of being alone. You are now an outcast. There is a great stigma attached because of your separation from the group. You feel guilty, as if you did something wrong, and that everyone else thinks you did something wrong. You feel alone.

### Peter gets UnChosen

I had risen to Executive Vice President of Global sales for a Swiss Multinational instrumentation company. I had taken my family to Zurich to live for four years. This was a great training ground, where I learned business, sales, management, marketing and corporate strategy. The company was one of the grandfathers of the old Swiss Industry and well-respected firm with over 150 years of continuous existence. I met many of my mentors and life-long friends here. It was a great experience. I traveled the world and returned to Pakistan to market into the growing textile industry there. My kids attended the international school of Zurich, which to this day brought a different perspective to their lives. My wife and I developed close friendships with the EX-Patriot community in Zurich. We were all close friends and our kids were everyone's kids. We all looked out for one another.

We were living our dream once again ten years later. Life was good. Life was so good that I received a promotion and my CEO wanted me to relocate to Knoxville, Tennessee at the America's HQ to take the new EVP job. I had an option to stay in Zurich and wish many times that I had stayed longer, mainly for my kids. It's hard to say no to job promotions.

The next four years were most trying and difficult I had seen. The textile industry faced a huge consolidation and many of the textile manufacturers, our clients were closing or moving to Asia. I had to lay off many of the colleagues that I had grown with. It was painful being the hatchet man. I had to downsize my team from over 200 to 80 employees. In a three-year period approximately two thirds of the textile plants in North America had disappeared, creating change for thousands of workers, executives and their families. A new exodus began to relocate to low cost countries like China, Vietnam, Pakistan and India. The market was turned upside down and shaken and so was my life. It was time for change again.

The company ownership also sold the company to us, the management team. I had conducted our first management buyout with a team of ten people and we purchased our instrument division from the ownership. One Friday afternoon, the CEO and two VP's that were my colleagues called me to the main conference room.

"Peter, you know that times are changing and we have to restructure our business. We thank you for your many years of service and will give you a generous severance package but we feel it is in the best interest for you to depart. You are effectively laid off and your position is being eliminated by December of this year." This was late October when I had heard this news. At this point, I really could not believe my ears and that my once esteemed colleagues had ousted me out the door.

I remember that day like it was yesterday. There was a feeling of complete shock and awe. I didn't know what to say. I looked at the three of them and left the room. I drove home to my wife, hugged her and began crying. I rarely am an emotional person but I was completely overwhelmed with grief. Later that grief turned to anger and later resentment. I was out of my cult. No more Christmas parties, no friendships at the office and no plan on what to do next. I was alone.

* * *

UnChosen comes in many ways, in many forms, with many different types of deliveries. The results are the same. A great feeling of being alone, embarrassed, ashamed, overwhelmed, confused, and depressed all at the same time.

## Chapter 3

## What the Hell Do I Do Now?

When you are UnChosen, you'll be sitting around asking yourself this question. It's a valid question. Other than 'why me?' it is the question overwhelming your mind and your existence. It is at the forefront of your thoughts. You cannot process anything else. You mentally cannot process the situation you have found yourself in at this point of life. You keep saying to yourself, "This is something that happens to other people." After years of stability, security, and an overall comfort level with your day to day routine, your world is now upside down. Your pattern of living has been broken. There is a lot to be done, and you have no idea where to start. You have never felt so lost and alone. Lost in a world you have never been in, and alone with your thoughts and your fears.

So, what do you do now? Lonely, afraid, and confused: if you are like most, you will get little direction or support from your boss or your human resources department at the company that let you go. They have probably never been through this, and like everyone else you know, cannot begin to realize the impact or empathize with you. Human Resource departments have also gone through a major overhaul throughout the years. They used to be a strong advocate for the employee. No longer. There is little contact or attempt by them to steward you through this transition.

You start trying to pick up the pieces. If you are fortunate like some and get career placement services provided for you, then you will at least have some support. If you are offered that support, take it! That will at least provide an opportunity to pull it all together with guided structure. If not, you will be relying on yourself, friends, family, and whoever else you can enlist. Given you have the financial ability you might consider engaging a career coach and placement resources yourself.

When you are UnChosen you feel like an outcast. You are discarded. You are no longer a member of the family. You have not been separated from a group you were this tight with since you graduated high school.

In so many ways you are alone. You feel alone because you think you are the only one that has experienced these emotions. You may have seen others that have gone through this, but they are most likely outwardly stoic, and will never reveal their pain. You think that what you are experiencing others have never experienced.

This has happened to you, and you feel that you alone must deal with it. Like so many other things in life, our pride makes us feel like we should be able to handle this. We don't know that everything we are struggling through in this situation has been felt by others. It has been a major source of pain for them, just like us.

In the end, it really is all up to you. No matter how you break it down, it all comes down to the fact that *you* will have to take action to fix this situation that you were now in. No one is going to fix it for you. And no one is really going to walk with you and hold your hand and tell you *what* to do along the way. Only people that have been through the same experience are going to understand how you are feeling, and the journey you are on.

But daily, the question remains, "What do I do now?" And if even you knew what to do, how would you do it in this mental state you are in?

Everyone's experience is different based on their age, their financial situation, the market they are in, and how quickly they can find a job. It will also depend on how resilient they are. The one thing most everyone has in common is that they experience an emotional impact and trauma.

### Peter Unprepared

> I had mixed emotions for the first week. I was mainly in shock and disbelief. I didn't have an office to go to in the morning. I didn't have my direct reports

calling me each hour talking about the next deal. I didn't communicate what had happened to anyone except my close friends and family. My colleagues and close friends were sending me their condolences. Those only made me feel worse.

I recall one conversation the second week with my former boss, who told me "Peter, you have now been set free." He had already departed the company moving to another division outside of textiles, because he had seen the crash coming. He was simply one of the most intelligent and visionary people that I have ever met. I didn't realize the wisdom of his comments at the time. But, yes, I had been "set free" from an industry that was spiraling downward and had no future. This was the silver lining in the clouds.

A week had passed and I was still numb and with mixed emotions. On the start of week two, I began to feel angry about what had happened. I received a call from one of my partners who offered me the opportunity to attend the ITMA (International Textile Machinery) trade show in Birmingham, England. He suggested this might be a good idea for networking and allowing me to look for a new job. I appreciated the gesture and after much thought accepted. At ITMA, I met all my agents, distributors and clients. It was a grand reunion and of course they all knew that I was leaving following the show. I realized at the show that textiles were shrinking and moving to Asia. I met several colleagues that were displaced and were at the show on their own expense networking for jobs. I realized at that point that I was exiting textiles, the industry that I knew so well, and would never be coming back.

The week at the trade show was emotionally difficult and draining. During those ten days, I learned to talk about my displacement to others and come out in the open. I developed a positive approach to strangers but still trashed the company to my good friends. I warned them all to be wary. Many of them would leave in the subsequent years. I started the networking process and practicing my elevator speech: who I was and my area of expertise. I had meetings with many of my good friends and listened to their advice. The company never sent me to an outsourcing or displacement service; I was on my own. I had never thought of looking for a new job and quite frankly didn't really know what process to follow.

I didn't have a plan nor did I have a strategy. I

didn't know what industry to go into next. However, I did know one thing. I was a sales and marketing executive and I understood the value of networking. I started talking to people and realized that being displaced was not an embarrassment or a bad thing altogether. It was simply a change. I felt lonely and lost with no one to coach me or assist me with my difficult situation. I was a seasoned salesman, one of the best in the textile industry; they called me "The Closer." If Peter Jones could not close the deal or smooth the client out, no one could. I used my instincts as a salesman and started doing what came naturally. Salesmanship. I had to find a new industry, a new company and sell myself again. The big red *reset* button has been pushed. I had to start over and close a deal for me!

\* \* \*

When you are UnChosen, you are scared. Scared of not finding employment. Scared of all the unknowns ahead of you. You are afraid you will not be able to bear the burden of this great weight that has been placed upon you. Afraid you will let your family and friends down, and afraid you will let yourself down. You are afraid that you will collapse.

If you are like most, you haven't searched for a job outside of your current company for years, and you probably don't have a current resume. You also have never been in this situation in your life where you have family and obligations and no job. When you are young and unemployed, it's a different world. Back then you only had yourself to take care of and to worry about. Now, staring at the space out in front of you, you think about your commitments, your family, and especially your children. How will you support them without income? You are visualizing the day not too far in the future when your money runs out. Life is rushing at you at an enormous pace, and just trying to process your situation is stress enough to cause you to emotionally break down. And you do.

There is also a loss of faith in yourself that begins to creep in on day one. Self-doubt is one of your greatest enemies from this point forward. Since you have been with a company so long, you start to wonder if your skills are transferable. You even begin to question if you have any marketable skills at all. You question the skills you used, and were successful with, day to day in your former job. Were you even good at what you did? Even if you were a high performer you will have self-doubt. In that environment of self-doubt, you question that you will be able to convince someone else that you can do the job. Worse than that, you realize that you will *have* to convince someone else that you have skills and can perform the duties of a job. It's like justifying your existence. How does a person go about doing that?

You sit around staring at the walls asking yourself "Why me?" but there is no answer to be found. The thing to understand now is that there will never be a good answer to that question. You need to make a resolution to look forward and not back. That is the best and only strategy at this point. Take a deep breath. Understand that you are going to be okay. One day at a time. It's easy to say and think, but terribly hard to do. At times, impossible.

That first day is one of many to come that will be mentally exhausting. You are mentally bombarded with problems that need to be solved, and at the same time coming to terms with the situation you are in. Money, job search, self-esteem, how do you tell your family, why did it have to be me, ego, savings, fear of the unknown, how to get together a plan of action, and how this is going to affect your life and retirement. In addition to all that add the feeling of being alone and scared to death. You also feel ashamed and worthless.

All of this is a heavy load. Your mind is trying to juggle it all, and make sense of it. To say that it is overwhelming is an understatement. When you lay down in bed at night all you have is your thoughts and fears. Thoughts and Fears. Why me? No answers come, and no rest or sleep comes.

Sleep will be scarce for many nights. Days and weeks go by without a complete night of rest. Your body is numb. Your mind will not let your body rest. It may be weeks, months, or years before restful and tranquil sleep will return.

The other possibility is excessive sleep. Depression may push you in the other direction entirely. Your escape may be sleep. You may struggle to get out of bed to even meet the day.

In addition to issues with sleeping, you cannot eat. Weight loss and no sleep. Two things your body needs most in this situation, proper rest and nourishment: you have neither, and you are totally exhausted.

Or maybe you are the type that deals with stress by eating. Eating, everything in sight. And it's not the healthy kind of eating. It's everything junk. In a few weeks the pounds are adding on and you feel lethargic and depressed. More eating ensues.

All these reactions are normal in this situation. Everyone will deal with this differently. It will most likely manifest in extremes.

Options. What are your options? What the hell do you do now? No, really. What the hell do you do now? In the midst of all this, you need, no you *have* to make decisions and get a plan to get back on track.

This is a terrible environment mentally to try to reason and make decisions. There is a tough road ahead.

### Greg & the Struggle

Months and months have passed by of motivating myself. I keep trying to keep myself upbeat and positive. Day after day of battling with myself, my ego, my self-worth, and keeping myself motivated to move forward and to stay positive. It's mentally draining. Mostly, it's just plain hard. It's really, really hard. Every day I live, everything I do, and everywhere I go, the experience I have and my level of happiness is all a matter of perspective. It's the lens I look through on a daily basis. Being UnChosen and the state of unemployment changes that lens. The lens is dark, and it's depressing.

Everything surrounding me reminds me that I'm unemployed, that I was UnChosen and no longer a part of something. No longer able to feel of value. Everything I see has dollar signs attached, reminding me that money is now finite. Everyone I meet is a reminder in some way that I am unemployed. Friends and family ask you if I have 'found' anything. "No, not yet" I reply in the best positive voice that I can muster. Some stop asking, and I battle within myself and wonder if I prefer they interrogate me with their silence, or if they go ahead and ask. Either way it is in the forefront of my thoughts. It's inescapable. Every business I see is a reminder of a place I might work, or where I won't be working. Or, it's just a reminder of all the people that DO have jobs there.

Every day is failure. My wife comes home and wants to hear good news today. Did you get a call back? Did you get a lead? Did you find any job postings? No, not today. Failure.

The simple fact of the matter is that being UnChosen is not a solo ride. As miserable and lonely as I feel, I know that my wife, and my children are along for the ride, and that just compounds the pressure I place on myself every day. My wife and I have built a life together, and now our life plans are upset. We are starting over.

*** 

You are UnChosen; UnChosen from your work family and friends, and from the place you have called home for many years, possibly decades.

You are just like many that are UnChosen. Like them, you have not had to find a job in many years, maybe decades. You're tired. You're depressed. You're alone. You're scared. And you have a daunting task ahead of you. You have a spouse and family to support, and you're not sure if you can even replace the salary you were making. The pressure is incredible. You are asking yourself, "What the Hell do I do now?"

## Chapter 4

## Trauma

There are certain things in life you begin to take for granted. After a long time in your job and with your company you take tomorrow for granted. It is embedded into your life, your schedule, and your short term and long term plans. It's a framework that you operate within personally as well as professionally. It is like the sun coming up in the morning; you take your job, your life, and your career for granted. Over time, you have developed a pattern of living based on your career that is comfortable.

Your pattern is broken now and there is darkness. You are alone, confused, afraid. No, you're scared to death. All you can think about is unemployment and no paycheck. How will the bills get paid, and the family be supported? There are many options that go through your head the day you are UnChosen and for days, weeks, and months to come. We wish we could tell you that they are all positive and uplifting. When you are in this position, you know how George Bailey feels in the movie *It's a Wonderful Life*. George is in a crisis situation and feels that he is worth more dead than alive because of his life insurance. He stands on the bridge ready to jump as he holds the life insurance policy in his hand contemplating his options.

When UnChosen, the thoughts go through your mind also about Life Insurance and how it will support the family, and how you will no longer have to deal with this situation any longer.

Greg's Mental State

That Wednesday night in February on the day I was UnChosen and continuing on through Thursday my brain continued to try and process what had just happened. Better yet, what I can do about it. My first thoughts were of supporting my family. For the first time in my life I had a wife and children and would soon have no income to support them. I thought of George Bailey standing on the bridge, with the insurance policy in hand. It's an option. It's an option that I begin to compute how many years all that insurance money will support my family, and what a good life they could still lead…without me. Without me. Those words were finally resonating in my head. Without me.

I can't. I cannot leave that legacy for my children. I cannot leave them the legacy of money and the fact that their husband and father was not strong enough to work this through. How could my children have pride in someone too weak to realize that money is not the core of my existence? Plus, I love them too much to leave them.

I recognize, like George, that suicide it is not a viable option. I am too strong for that, and I love life, God, and my family.

Breaking through that barrier, however, does not remove the fear. I am in a situation that I have never been in before. There is nothing in life that has prepared me for where I am, or where I'm going. I am absolutely terrified as I move through this dark place in my life, and equally terrified of the journey ahead to get out.

\* \* \*

The brain in this UnChosen state is locked down. There are too many problems coming at you to be able to process them all. Job hunt, resume, interviewing, paying the bills, and on top of all that, the stigma attached to your situation. What will others think? Better yet, where do you begin? How do you prioritize all these things? Where do you start on these things that you have never had to do before, and really don't know how to do? All these things lock down your body and your mind.

### Greg Physically Unwell

The first night there was no sleep at all. After two weeks have passed there is still little sleep each night for me. My mind continues to race and try to solve the problem. What did I do wrong? What could I have done differently that would have prevented this?

Sleep. If I could just sleep. If I could just rest. My body can't rest because my brain can't rest. I have laid awake each night wondering why me, and what to do next.

I also cannot eat. Eating makes my stomach hurt. It makes me physically sick. In less than two weeks I have dropped at least 10 pounds from not eating. It's okay, because this situation has taken my appetite. I'm not hungry.

At the end of the second month, I still have not slept a full night through, and wonder if I ever will again. I am north of 15 pounds in weight loss. I'm eating to some extent, but not in normal amounts, and it is still not easy to do. For the most part I am forcing myself to eat.

## UnChosen

* * *

Alice Park reported in a Time Magazine article in 2009 that studies showed job loss definitely affects our health. Park found "that among people unemployed under these circumstances and who did not report any health problems prior to losing their job, 80% were diagnosed with a new health problem." She reported that "all of this serves as a strong reminder that losing one's job can be a trauma — for both body and mind, and one that may have lasting effects."

If physical problems aren't bad enough, the mental anguish alone is stifling. Loneliness, fear and confusion all work in unison to extort your mind to the dark side. They can be your friend or your enemy. Confusion causes delays and results in second guessing. Delay in decisions destroys the ability to create ideas and creates chaos. You will realize that you are not an expert in dealing with confusion and chaos that has been dealt to you. People generally don't know how to deal with chaos and confusion. You have to experience it, take hold of it, and learn from it. It's like on the job training. Some things there are no other avenues to learn. You have been dealt a nice dose of confusion and chaos. You will have to learn how to deal with it.

Confusion translates to uncertainty and re-evaluation.

Once UnChosen, you begin to question your skills, your abilities, your self-esteem, and your life in general.

### Greg's Mental State

In the first days after I was UnChosen I am generally in a state of shock. My mental capacity is being stifled by all the problems that lay ahead that keep circling in my head. Part of it is the inability to really accept that this has happened. I can't process it. I have poured everything I am into the company, and now I am on the street.

Another major source of stress is money, and how will we survive as a family. Everything we consume has dollar signs on it now. I remember vividly standing at my vanity in the bathroom putting contacts in that first week and looking at the $3 bottle of contact solution. Dollar signs spin in my head as I realize there may come a day that I cannot even afford to purchase a replacement bottle of solution.

I try to keep upbeat, but inside I am an absolute wreck. I have trouble being alone. I have trouble being with people. I don't know what to say. I don't know what to do.

UnChosen

\*\*\*

The emotional rollercoaster ride is just beginning, and the trauma train has just left the station for an unknown destination.

<u>Peter's Ride</u>

Three weeks pass since the termination of my Social Contract. I experienced an entire round of emotions. There was the shock and dismay of the initial job loss of the first week. During week two, shock led to anger and blaming of others for my problems. During week three while at ITMA, I began my therapy of talking of people and starting to admit that I had to take ownership of my problem. The anger and jealousy would last for many weeks following. I don't recall how many but it lasted several months. I still think about it with fonder memories now years later. My anger provided motivation and allowed me to move forward. I would show my colleagues that I can find another better opportunity. I would be successful again. I would win again!

\*\*\*

# Part 2

# The Journey

## Chapter 5

## Who Am I Anyway?

The first step in your journey is toward restoring personal identity. Yesterday, you had a job, and an identity. Today, you are no longer a part of an organization or have a job. You no longer have co-workers or a group to identify with. You don't have a job, and you don't have an identity outside of the workforce. You never realized how important a job and a job title is to your identity is in this society until now. And it is not just what you do and your job title, it's also a matter of *where* you did your job. People generally associate their identity and borrow their credibility, esteem, and pride from what they do, and the company they do it for. We have grown up in a society where our life's fulfillment is predicated on our job or work. Self-worth is derived from what we do. Self-esteem comes from what we do, and at times even more so the company we work for; especially if that company is perceived as being prestigious.

"What do you do?" It's a popular question wherever you go and talk to people. When you are employed you have an answer. I'm a Key Account Manager, a Plumber, an Accountant, an IT Manager, at X company. If you only answer with your job title, the follow-up question is "Where do you work?" The more prestigious the title or company, the more proudly you deliver the response. "I work for Coca-Cola," or "I work for IBM" are generally followed with that wow response from the one who has enquired. Your chest grows with pride as if you owned the company.

Today, you don't have an answer to either of those two most popular questions. And you are simply terrified of being asked. You're embarrassed and ashamed at the answer you have to give. "I was laid off," is what you are feeling inside and you want to say it out loud so badly and share your pain. "I was let go," resonates in your brain and the emotional strain from being ashamed is overwhelming. Any way you slice it, it's a hard message to deliver to other people and hold your head high. Your self-worth right now is zero.

You need to keep telling yourself that you inherently have not changed. Not one thing about you has changed except that you don't have a job. But in our society, a job, a trade, and an active career is *everything*. Isn't it? At least we perceive it that way. Therefore, you don't have an identity. It *is* your identity. It is your credibility. It is everything.

Career coaches will tell you to make being laid off a non-event. Answer the question with something like this: "As many companies are doing these days, there was a re-

## UnChosen

organization and I was impacted during that re-organization. I'm currently looking for an opportunity." This is a great way to positively respond during an interview, and it works in social situations. However, at first it doesn't help you feel much better inside.

The further you get from that last day at work, the harder your identity is to keep. Your self-confidence begins to waiver more and more. The longer you are unemployed, the harder it is to be confident about your abilities and skills. The more you scramble to find work, the more scrambled your identity becomes.

So really, who are you? In the end isn't it true that who you are as a person has to be greater than the sum of what you do and where you do it. Life has to be greater than that. "I have to be more than that," you think. Ego. This darn thing called and ego. If you can just get that ego out of the way to let yourself think. Can you separate the person from the job title? Can you separate skills, talents, your core competencies and capabilities out from the job description or job duties? If you can do this, you can find identity and self-worth again.

### Greg & Identity

Weeks have passed now since I left my job. I have come to a point in life where living without a clear identity is like trying to live without air. It's suffocating. When you have signed onto the Social Contract and transitioned your mind from a job to a career mentality, your position and title are everything. Twenty-two years and I was a company man. I was a Coca-Cola employee and darn proud of it. I was proud of my group, co-workers, and peers and the work we were doing. I was proud of my work.

As of now I don't have that and for many weeks now I have not landed a job. People continue to ask me what I do. What do I do? Well, when I can sleep, I wake up in the morning in mental anguish over just how to answer that very question. "What do you do?"

Right now I feel that it will be weeks and months before I am comfortable talking to people about my 'situation.' And weeks and months before I am comfortable presenting an identity outside the realm of my job and company that is now in the past.

The incredible thing is that most people want to help, and most don't understand what I do, and I will have to learn how to help them, help me.

*　*　*

You really do have to learn how to help people help you.

## UnChosen

One thing is for sure, unless they have been through the experience, they will never be able to understand how you feel.

People will keep asking you what you do. And you will keep trying to answer the question. And although you may come up with a well-groomed and coherent answer that will make perfect sense to them, such as "I'm in transition," the inner pain will remain until you can resolve this internally. You will need to come to grips with your situation and detach what you do from defining you fully as a person.

### Peter & Identity

In western society we often identify ourselves with our job, position or status. I had to look in the mirror and find my identity. I was still my old self, with the same skills and outlook on life. So, what was different? I told myself that I am unique and for the same reasons that I was successful in my previous jobs is the same reason why someone will hire me again. I came to realize that I have a certain skill set that is unique and an attitude to generate revenue for organizations. I had to define myself and create my brand image. Finally, I realized that I had to separate my job from my persona. They were two different things. My friends, family and close friends didn't like me because I was an executive Vice President or geo-political advisor, but because I was Peter Jones.

I finally realized that jobs come and go and my persona is really a product of those lessons and experiences acquired from life and business. Those are the things that set me apart and could get new organizations interested in me again.

\* \* \*

The first thing you have to realize is that these days being UnChosen is a very common occurrence. "I'm in transition," "I was impacted during a reorganization," or even "I was laid off" do not carry the severe stigma as in days past. As the "The Social Contract" is diminishing and changing the workplace, so has the commonplace occurrence of layoffs diminished the stigma attached.

Secondly, understand that people really do want to help you. Not all people, but you will be pleasantly surprised at how many want to jump on board with you and help on the journey.

Lastly, *you* have not changed. The answer to "Who am I?" is inside you. There is a greater and more fulfilling peace inside you when you realize who you are outside the confines

## UnChosen

of your job and the company. There is power inside you and the ability to stand alone. Once you tap into that, your confidence and personal power are greater than they ever were when you borrowed your credibility from a job or company.

## Chapter 6

# What am I worth?

This is the really hard part, as if anything you experience during the UnChosen experience is easy. What are people willing to pay for you for your knowledge and experience? Let's get the white elephant out into the middle of room: they are probably not going to pay you what you made with your previous employer. It's possible, but not likely. The longer you have stayed with a company or in a position, the more you have most likely outpriced yourself in the market. It will also depend upon your willingness and ability to relocate yourself and your family for an opportunity.

Peter's Pay Struggle

Let's face it, the biggest failure in corporations today is the human resources department. They should rename this to the "cover your ass department." They exist only to keep the peace and prevent lawsuits. The job of creating talent and the acquisition of talent resides in the hands of the managers in each department. In my case, a vice president reports to a President or CEO, so my fate rested in reaching those people. Looking at websites with pay scales is also helpful. However, I never really learn what I am worth until I interview for a position. It is all dependent on many factors and variables. I lived in a city with a relatively small international sales marketing market. In order to continue my lifestyle and pay scale from my previous employer, I had to look at job markets globally. Luckily, one of my mentors and my old boss told me that there were 2 million people commuting for their job from one city or region to another. My next door neighbor did turnarounds from the US to Nigeria every 30 days, commuting for an Oil & Gas company. My wife and I had children in high school and middle school and they needed stability. Moving was possible but would be difficult. I had already made twenty-two corporate moves. My boss taught me something very profound – "If they like you then they will let you commute and they will hire you. But get that interview."

So, finding my worth was an exercise in trial and error. It was all highly dependent on the sacrifices that I and my family were willing to make.

* * *

As much as your identity is driven by what you do and where you do it, so is your self-worth. It is amazing how much a person relates self-worth to a job title and the amount of money they make, or that might be perceived that they make. We are all very shallow in that area.

There is also value when you are Chosen, and part of a team. When you are UnChosen, intentionally selected and removed from the team, you instantly feel a loss of value. You feel worthless. As much as we would like to fight it, we measure ourselves by our job title, the money we make, and the lifestyle that we can provide for our family. At the very basic level, self-worth starts with having a job in this western society. It shows that the skills and abilities we have are worth something to someone. In addition to that, the feeling of accomplishment that we get from doing the job provides its own level of value. There's a sense of pride and self-worth in our ability to be a subject matter expert. In the context of a job, that value and worth exists. Some companies and managers call that 'adding value.' When you get up in the morning and have nowhere to go, nowhere to add value, when you have nothing to do, you feel worthless.

### Greg's First Day of Joblessness

Seven thirty in the am and the normal morning

routine. I got up out of bed at six thirty, took a shower, got dressed, got the kids out of bed, and prepared for the day. Everyone is buzzing around as they normally do. I am felling kind of lost. I have nowhere to go to today.

My wife is putting lunches together and preparing for her work day ahead. It is 7:30 now and everyone is ready to go out the door. It's the normal routine on an abnormal day for me and for the family. I have a lot to do today but it has nothing to do with my old job of yesterday. I don't have a job to go to. My job today and every day forward is to find a job. Today I am lost and feeling worthless.

I'm sitting at the kitchen table as everyone is going out the door to school and work. My wife turns and looks at me. I must be a sight. Based on the look I get it must be like looking at someone that just found out they were terminal with cancer. Or maybe like someone just shot my beloved dog. No, they shot my self-esteem and self-worth. They killed it.

"Are you okay?" she asks. Or maybe it was "are you going to be okay?" I can't remember exactly.

"Yes." I reply trying to convince her, and convince myself. But nothing today is okay. This will be the routine for weeks, and months to come. There are many more of those looks in my future.

*** 

On the day you are UnChosen, you will walk out of the workplace knowing your paycheck is soon to be gone. Your self-worth, along with your financial worth is about to go to zero.

You feel used and discarded. You really feel worthless. You no longer know how to value yourself. At least you can no longer value yourself based on perceived conventional terms in this society. Inside you know nothing else has changed about you other than your job. People are going to ask you what you do. "I do nothing," you will think on the inside, "and that has no value."

<u>Greg's Battle</u>

From the first day I became unemployed I was scared to death about being able to replace my salary. And rightly so. Statistics show that most that are laid off are in store for 25% cut in pay when they are able to return to the workforce. I was very fortunate that we have over the years lived within our means, and we have had resources and savings. I was also fortunate that a generous severance package was provided by the company. Unfortunately, that does not solve all the problems. Jobs do not grow on trees, and senior level management jobs are scarce. Especially in the small market that I am in. Not that being in a larger market would have helped tremendously. I know people that have been UnChosen in a large market and took almost 2 years to land a new position.

I have always prided myself in treating everyone the same, no matter how much money they made, or what job they had. I always have liked to think I treat all people as just people. Now I am unable to give myself that same level of grace. I am judging my own self-worth by my lack of employment and income. Worse than that, I'm scared about the future and my ability to make money, and the thought that my next role might not be as 'prestigious' as the last.

\* \* \*

For decades people in the workforce have been riding the good wave and were fortunate to have worked during a period when companies were providing good benefits packages including a pension plan, 401k, and medical benefits that didn't involve the employee having to meet a high deductible each year. Salaries and benefits are down. We are clearly not worth what we were as an employee in years past. As a matter of fact, on the day you are UnChosen, it is like driving a new car off the lot. As soon as you are off the lot, you have depreciated in value, for no reason at all. You are unchanged, except in value in the workplace.

There are some very fortunate people that are UnChosen and land better financially. That is not typical these days for most lose 20 percent on average of their salary and benefits when they are able to land again. Better pay or not, they will still be traumatized, and hurt by the loss of their work family and being UnChosen from the team.

To solve the "What am I worth?" problem, we are going to have to look deeper inside ourselves. We are going to have to become less shallow and start asking ourselves better and more relevant questions about our personal mission and our existence. Is it only what we do, where we do it, and how much we are paid that defines our worth? No. We need to look deep, look at our relationships and our lives and be able to value ourselves on a different measurement system. Only then can we begin to recover. We also need to believe in ourselves and our skills that have not changed since we were UnChosen. We can still do *all* those things that we did before. We have to recognize that we have competencies and skills

## UnChosen

and value them on their own merit. Most importantly we have to value those competencies and skills ourselves.

We *have* to do those things and crawl out of this abyss of non-value and be able to face people. Especially as we prepare for interviewing. We *have* to feel like we are worth something, or the interviewer will smell our fear, self-doubt, and lack of confidence; and that will kill our chances of getting hired.

The two components of the "What am I worth?" question will need to be dealt with separately, and together. The monetary side will need some planning as you evaluate your spending, lifestyle, and plans for the future. Realizing that your income could go up, go down, or stay the same is part of your financial plan that will need some attention. Talking with your family and a financial planner can get you on the right road.

On the other side of the coin (no pun intended) is the personal feeling of self-worth you are battling. As you battled the "Who am I?" question this was certainly a part of that struggle. It's the same but different. As you wrestle with this, you have to dig deep into your personal value system and determine that who you are and what you are worth is *not* defined in monetary terms. Your value as a person, a human being, does not boil down to dollars and cents.

## Chapter 7

## Am I Relevant and Marketable?

The day has come and you are UnChosen. As you begin to develop your plan, you may look around and find that what you do is not as marketable as you thought. There are many trades, skills, and job titles that fall cleanly and neatly into buckets. However, there are also many that don't. If you are an accountant, it is likely that you will look through job postings and find similar job titles and descriptions you will feel comfortable with, and comfortable applying for. Your skills and resume will make perfect sense for those positions. If you are a "Sales Process Analyst," you are probably not going to find a large volume of jobs with that exact title listed on job sites across the web. So the job search begins along with your struggle to fit yourself into other job titles and other job roles.

After a long engagement with your last company you now have a somewhat shocking reality to face. Your long time employer has done a very good job of teaching you how to be successful 'inside' their organization. They invest in you only to the extent that it will help them. There is a fine line between companies investing in you to be successful and productive

## UnChosen

for them, and investing in what they perceive would create you as a flight risk. Many are not placing priority on certifications and formal training for that very reason. There are exceptions where certifications are a must, but those are isolated. Even as the book *Who Moved My Cheese?* hit the market and well-meaning Human Resource employees and managers were distributing the propaganda, they continued to operate their organizations in the same manner. They continued to develop people to be successful inside the organization. They knew they were going to move the cheese.

*Who Moved My Cheese?* presents the idea that where you have always gotten your 'cheese' is not always where you will find it. Cheese is used as a metaphor for your livelihood, your substance, otherwise known as your paycheck. *Who Moved My Cheese?* was telling us The Social Contract was about to expire.

Okay. Let's be fair. It is not their job to make you successful outside of their organization. The main idea that people missed during the *Who Moved My Cheese?* movement was that it was up to the employee to keep themselves relevant in the market and keep themselves trained, up to date, and certified. If you missed this queue, you were not alone. Everyone was still living with the idea that they had "The Social Contract" in their back pocket.

## Greg's Revelation

It's funny, because I always told the people that worked in my group to be ready for what was probably inevitable. I always thought I was ready if the phone call ever came. I was seriously mistaken.

I placed my heart and my soul into my work and the company. I built my world between my job, my church, and my family. For 22 years that was my world. No clubs, no business associations, and no civic groups. I came to find that I had not even built a personal network of business contacts and friends inside my own town because I worked for an international company.

One of the raw brutal truths that I had to face upon hitting the street was that I was no longer relevant in the outside world. I was doing a great job at knowing what to do and how to do it within the company, but I, nor the company spent any time or resources developing me to be of value anywhere else. I didn't have any certifications or degrees. I had not attended a workshop outside the company in more than 10 years. I was not built for success outside of my role, nor outside of the company.

I am not pointing blame at the company, because I

am certainly as much or more responsible for the situation I found myself in. However, I was also a 'company man' and poured my heart and soul into my job and the company, and only my job and the company. And by the way, the company let me.

I was counting on 'The Social Contract.' I didn't take time for business, technical, civic, or association meetings or clubs. I was fully engaged within, and not focusing on any external foundation to build upon the day I was UnChosen. Because of the Social Contract that I thought existed, I didn't think I needed to. I should have seen the signals. My company, along with many others, cut funding for travel to seminars, events, and training many years ago. The only thing that was left was tuition reimbursement, and there was no way with the travel schedule and work schedule to ever try to be successful working the job and trying to get another degree; or at least that's what I thought. That's because I always put the company first, instead of putting me first. The end product was, I lost my relevance, and my marketability. My priorities were not in order.

When I first hit the street I was a dinosaur. I was outdated so badly I smelled of moth balls. I had no street smarts at all when it came to job search. I didn't know where to begin. I had no idea if I was even marketable in the current job market. Jobs of the type, title, and duties weren't just posted on every street corner for consideration; quite the contrary.

* * *

As the bond between you and the company develops and grows stronger, your focus on success in your role and growth within the company grows laser focused. The longer you are there, the stronger "The Social Contract" solidifies in your mind. This begins and is so gradual you won't notice. As you pass seniority milestones the feeling that your engagement will be eternal will become more real and cemented in your existence. Five years, then ten years pass, and as this happens, your journey to irrelevance in the job market has begun.

Relevance in the workplace is a real concern. It should always be at the forefront of your career strategy and personal development strategy. The guy that repaired typewriters in the 1960s and the 1970s had to get his head out of the sand and realize that the computer age was upon him in the 1980s. The typewriter was on the way out. Job skill relevance is real and tangible.

# UnChosen

## Peter Explores Relevance

When, I was UnChosen I felt that I was not relevant. I felt I didn't matter any longer because my previous employer didn't need me.

After much soul searching I realized yes, I am relevant, because I'm unique and I have skills. I am my own man and I can do this. An attitude adjustment is what I needed. I had to create my attitude first before I could begin to learn the answer to the question "Am I marketable?"

Someone, some company out there needs my skills and abilities. Somewhere out there is a company that matches my value system. I realized I had to keep looking until that moment when you make that connection. When you find that company or person that shares your vision and needs you. One man's trash is truly another man's treasure. There are many organizations out there that want and need my skills. I just had to find them. I am relevant, I am marketable. Simply because I am unique and there is no one else on this planet like me.

\* \* \*

Relevance is also a state of mind. Once you have measured

your skills against the job market and found you still have marketable skills, don't let your brain devalue your relevance in this world and in the job market.

### Greg Gets Some Advice

"On day one my wife and I sat down and talked through our new situation. Some of the first words out of her mouth were 'This is an opportunity that you would have never created for yourself.' Inside I knew she was right. I would have never left Coca-Cola.

Only until much later on did I really understand what this meant, and what it should mean to me. I finally figured out that creating opportunity for myself meant not becoming stagnant in life and career. It meant investing in myself and staying relevant.

\* \* \*

Staying relevant is recreating yourself constantly. Staying fresh mentally through self-development and training. Create opportunity through improving yourself mentally and physically. Watch the job market and make sure you know what the trends are for skills. Keep your skills and yourself relevant. Don't be like the typewriter repair man.

## Chapter 8

## Family, Friends, and Ghosts

No matter your age, your length of time in the workplace, or your job, you have many people in your life that are important to you. We are all fortunate and blessed with family and friends of varying degrees of personal relationships. When you were UnChosen you left the station on the trauma train and you will start looking for those that will go on the journey with you. These people will be essential in your journey for many reasons. They will support you emotionally, financially, spiritually, and support you in finding your new job. At least you hope so.

In the early hours and days of being UnChosen you will start trying to assemble a list of people in your brain that need to be on the train. Then you will start making some phone calls. People will really come to your rescue, and try to help in the best ways they know possible. It is truly inspiring and humbling.

Greg Reaches Out

It's a Sunday and we are at Church. It has been less than two weeks since I received the phone call and was

UnChosen. I am still walking around in a funk. As I sit in church, I feel like people can look at me and tell I'm unemployed. I am a mess. Mostly I just don't want to interact or talk with people because I still do not really know what to say or what to do. I really feel like I should not engage people until my mental state is better.

As I composed my list of people in the first day or two the thing I realized was that to get through this I needed to talk to someone that had done it. Someone that had transitioned successfully in the past.

I approached Peter after church and tried with all my might to hold the tears back as I told Peter my story of the prior week and what had happened and where things stood today. As I told the story, Peter looked at me thoughtfully, and caringly. When I was finished, there was a short pause. Peter grew a large smile on his face. His next words will walk with me forever in my life. Here I am in pain, almost in tears, and Peter is smiling. Peter says, "Man, you have been set free."

Peter's calmness that day was the beginning of understanding that I will recover. Understanding that I will survive. Somehow deep down I knew I would be okay. However, it would be months before I really understood Peter's comment.

Peter also invited me to lunch that week, to help coach me on next steps. One of the great first steps in the right direction on the journey.

*\*\*\**

Sometimes the most astounding help and support will come from the most unexpected places. You will never know where the most valuable support will come from during this period of pain.

Peter & the Relationship Experience

There are two levels of relationships that I experienced. People were either friends that were relatively sympathetic or they were indifferent to my situation. At the end of the day, I owned my situation and no else did. I had to get myself out of this rabbit hole. I figured out pretty quickly who were the friends that could help but the true realization is that most of my friends couldn't help me. Some offered help and others only provided encouragement. I realized again that basically I was on my own. However, my friends had value and that was networking. I made sure to tell all my friends I was looking for new opportunity. I followed up on any lead that I was given. You never know who you are going to meet.

The backbone of the unemployment is your family. They are the only ones that can empathize and relate. During these times my kids were young and didn't really understand. Even when they got older into their teens and into college they didn't understand. I really tried to keep my frustrations secret from the kids as they didn't need the stress nor the bother. Family provided comfort and hospitality because every day out there on the job search was the opposite. It is not an inviting environment.

Then came the ghosts. These are the people that appeared when you didn't expect to be there, and those that disappeared that you thought were your best friends. These are surprises in life. Here I discovered who were truly friends and who just acquaintances. The ghosts that appeared were a pleasant surprise and provided value because they volunteered to help. The ghosts that disappeared were disappointing to me, if not devastating. It was evidence of a relationship that really didn't exist on the level that I thought.

\* \* \*

UnChosen

Family is tremendously important to the journey. It's important that they are understanding and supportive. Friends are just as important. You probably have friends that you are closer to in life than most of your family. Especially those relationships that you have built at work. After all, you probably spend more time with co-workers than you do family or most of your friends. Relationships that you have built at work are extremely important.

In addition to those times when people are incredibly helpful, compassionate, and ever present, there will be times during this journey you are going to experience severe disappointment and abandonment. Some will disappear like ghosts. You will look around, and they are not to be found.

### Greg's Best Friend at Work

The day I was given notice that I was UnChosen, I finished with my phone call with my boss, packed up my things, and left work for the day. As I pulled out of the parking lot my first phone call was to my wife. I let her know what was going on, how our life was about to change. She was supportive, compassionate, and said we would talk later when she got home from work.

My second phone call was to someone I cherished as a colleague, but more as a friend. We were hundreds of miles apart, but at any meetings and after work functions, we were always together. I considered him my brother on many levels.

That day he was as shocked to hear the news as I had been. In the coming days and weeks I would look to him for support, comfort, and care. I'm sad to say that he was not there. As I approached my last days and began my first days of no job to go to, I kept expecting the phone to ring. It didn't ring. I reached out to him a couple times, and expected to get fulfillment and the return on the investment I had made in him emotionally over that last few years.

In the weeks and months to come, I would still look for Rick to call. Nothing. I am sad even today to think that the relationship was so fragile as the separation of me from the company would sever the strong bond into a weak and casual relationship. Rick turned into a ghost. He became invisible to me.

When I was UnChosen, there were several people like Rick that as I was sure would be by my side and never leave me. I believed they would be there calling me, supporting me, comforting me, and carrying me at times when I needed to be carried. I expected they would be there to help me back to a better mental place. They were gone, disappeared like ghosts.

\* \* \*

Ghosts. These people that we look to support us, even to carry us at times. We think they have our back and will be behind us fully a hundred percent of the time. We look around behind us and they are gone. They turned into ghosts.

Then fortunately there are ghosts of another kind. There are those that reveal themselves to you. You are going to experience a lot of incredible things on your journey. Understanding relationships better is one of them. Fortunately, there will be more high points in your journey with relationships than low points. As there are people that will disappear like ghosts, there are people that have been on your peripheral that you really have never seen before. You never really viewed them as committed friends or colleagues who would go to great lengths to help you emotionally and to help you find a new stop in your life and career. They are there, and some will make grand appearances and provide unbelievable support in a time of great need.

<u>Greg's New Connection & Revelation</u>

About the second week of unemployment I received a call from someone I knew as a business acquaintance only. I had done a lot of business with his company and really had not connected with him on a personal level at all. Joe called me that second week and asked how I was doing and mentioned several companies he thought I should consider applying with, including his.

Being in the state I was in, I was very thankful for the call and was still not in the right mental state to understand and appreciate what is was that he was offering.

In about two weeks Joe called again. Same type of conversation of how I was doing and again with some lists of companies that he felt I would be a fit for. I was starting to begin to be impressed and confused. How could I have ever missed connecting with such a great person in the course of my work and social life? Here was a person that had nothing to gain from helping me beyond personal satisfaction. I really did not understand what was happening at the time.

By the time Joe reached out on the third occasion I really began to understand the importance of what was happening. It was also the beginning of really understanding people, relationships, and how I missed something during my career and my personal life.

We talked about prospective companies again and I

asked to get together with him for lunch. After lunch with Joe I began to realize just how brilliant he was and what a great opportunity I had missed in my interactions with him in the past. I had only viewed him as a vendor, a salesman. I'm ashamed to say, outside of that I had really not thought about him at all.

During the course of the next two years Joe would continue to encourage me, bring me to sporting events where there was opportunity to meet key people with other companies, get me an interview with his company, and eventually get me hired with his company.

Joe came from nowhere. He was a different kind of ghost in my life. He was right in front of me. I never really saw him until he revealed to me what a caring person he was, and what a valuable resource he was in supporting me mentally and in my job search.

\* \* \*

Many people will pass through your lives. During this time of trial and transition, you become more aware of relationships than you ever have before in your life. You become more aware of feelings than you ever had before in your life. As you begin to analyze your relationships you begin to see people much differently. You watch friends and family turn to ghosts. You watch ghosts that were taken for granted in the past materialize into valued friends.

Relationships are a constant flow in your life. Remember that valued relationships take commitment from both sides. They cannot be a one-way street. It's important you realize you cannot just be a taker. You must enter every conversation and every relationship asking yourself what you can do for that person; how you can help them. Only then will the relationship prosper. Even with all that in place, relationships are fluid. People are going to come and go in their natural cycle.

## Chapter 9

## How Do I Talk to People?

After the initial shock and trauma of being UnChosen, the realization will set in that you are going to have to meet and interact with people. Nothing has change about you personally on the exterior, but the lens that you are viewing the world through has changed. You feel like a leper not just in the social sense, but the physical sense. You feel like everyone can now see the physical scars of your situation and your mental state, just as if you had the disease. You feel everyone is staring at you, and they know you are about to break down at any moment and cry.

Your self-esteem is at rock bottom. The embarrassment of it all is overpowering, and you feel an inferiority to anyone and everyone you meet. You have no idea how you are going to talk to people in this state of mind. You are terrified at the thought of even seeing people.

Years of training in the business world and the ability to talk to people in difficult situations, to talk to senior level managers, customers, vendors, or colleagues can never quite prepare you for this. There is nothing in the world that can prepare you for this. You have no experience in this new and strange world you have been thrown into. Emotions are running high, and your ability to function normally is severely diminished.

There is great feeling of loss of power and self-worth. The feeling of inferiority is crushing to your ego. All the pride of what you have done and accomplished is now tarnished. At least that is the way you perceive it. Pride in yourself is one of those things that is hardly noticed until it is gone. When that happens, you keep telling yourself that what you did was valuable, but it's lost now somewhere deep inside you, overshadowed by this terrible new feeling of worthlessness.

The stigma attached to job loss is enormous, especially for the Baby Boomer generation and Generation X. These generations valued commitment and loyalty. They valued a career which involved a long engagement with the same company. Those that gained seniority earned a certain respect for their knowledge of the industry, the company, and the workplace. They were looked up to by others, and looked to for their advice and expertise.

Many are UnChosen these days. It has become commonplace, but the stigma remains. The feeling remains. The challenge to cope with it and talk with others remains.

# UnChosen

## Greg & Talking to People

I have no idea how I am going to face people. What will I say to them? I am so ashamed of the situation I am in and that I was UnChosen. Somehow I have to tell people that I no longer have a job, and I am fully ashamed of that even though I did not cause it. I am ashamed even when I know I should not be.

When I first try to talk to people about being jobless and ask them for help, I feel belittled, ashamed, and inferior. It's worse than the feeling you had when you were a child and you had to ask permission to do the most mundane things.

In the first days and weeks I am physically sick, weak, and mentally drained. I don't want to be in crowds. I don't want to see people. I don't want to have to interact. But there is no escaping it. I can't just isolate myself, or I will never be able to recover. The first few days when I go out in public and talk with friends and family it is all I can do to hold back my emotions. Tears are reluctantly withheld. I can withhold the tears, but not the feeling inside that people can see my pain and suffering.

I also know the 'what do you do?' question is lurking when I meet new people. I don't have a clue how to answer that question except 'I don't do anything.' 'I am worthless, I'm unemployed, and I don't have a clue what to do next!' That's what I really want to say.

* * *

Talking about job loss is not only difficult but it's an exercise in humility. It's an exercise in the positive when internally you struggle think about anything but the negative. You are feeling beaten and inferior. You feel as if you have been thrown out to the street and that no one really cares.

### Peter's Story

It became time to tell my story. Herein lies the problem. I was embarrassed to tell my story. That I had been fired, let go, UnChosen from my company. I knew that I had to start networking to get leads for jobs. My sales instinct kicked in but my desire to tell people was diminished. I couldn't motivate myself to tell people. It was a hard task because it caused embarrassment. I hated to tell people that I got laid off. So, guess what? I didn't tell them the real story. I told them the spin. "Well, John you know I spent great years with my company, but then industry we served crashed around us." "Plants were closing right and left. The only option was for me to move to China. I got tired of moving and took my severance plan and exited gracefully". So, I'm looking for new opportunities in international sales & marketing. I know how to grow companies, expand markets. I'm really good at sales, networking and managing leadership teams. This became my elevator speech. I practiced in in front of the mirror. I condensed it to two or three minutes. Short enough to keep someone's attention and long enough to give them a good understanding of what I was looking to do.

\* \* \*

Your personality profile will play a large role in how you will be able talk to people. Even for those that are more social, there is generally a tendency to focus on the negative and not on the positive things. During this time, the negative needs to stay in your head and your words should only reflect the positive. The more you say and hear positive words from your own mouth, the quicker you will begin to heal.

Practice makes perfect. Fine tune your message to people. Tell them what a great experience you had rather than how negative your boss or industry was. Talk to people positively. These are the same people that are going to refer to another person or job. These are the people that control your future.

The same applies for written communication. Articulate your message positively in both written and verbal form.

<u>Peter & Talking to People</u>

> During my job search, I remember helping others while they were unemployed. Sharing your contacts and job opportunities with others that you have found will get you a lot of points. I believe in good karma and that all you do that is positive will come back to you. Helping others is a good thing to do. Tell people your story and what you have learned. Tell them you are excited about the possibilities and what the future will hold. Use the unknown as a positive. Even if in your dark side your mind is telling your something else. Don't succumb to that part of your brain. Darkness will bring you down and will never let you see the light. Keep up the positive.

\* \* \*

In real estate they say the most important thing is location, location, location. When it comes to talking to people it is practice, practice, practice. There is no way to become comfortable except to learn the skill in the same way you learn

## UnChosen

any other skill, through practice. You are going to make mistakes. Give yourself grace to make mistakes, learn from them and get better. Keep it positive and keep moving forward.

## Chapter 10

## How Do I Tell My Story?

So now you have mustered up the nerve to go out in public, face people, and talk to them. What in the world will you say? Should you tell them your story, and if so, how do you tell them your story?

When you have a job your story is easy. You can tell people about what you do and where you work, and even the people that you work with. Now your world is upside down and you no longer have that story to tell. That story ended abruptly, without the ending that you had imagined. Just telling people that you no longer have a job seems like a monumental task emotionally. The words "I was laid off," sound so negative, so demeaning.

<u>Greg's Fear of Talking to People</u>

>I've started talking with people but I'm still not really sure what to say, or how to say it. Outside I am the same, but inside I don't feel like the same person. I'm not who I was anymore. At least that is the story I am telling myself inside. I don't recall in my life when I have been more embarrassed to talk to people. It's like I

did something wrong and now I must account for it. At first I am filled with the need to justify the event and why in particular it happened to me. I do this even when I do not know the answer to why it had to happen to me.

I am afraid of every encounter. I pray that no one will ask me what I do. At first when this happens I fumble. I stall. I get emotional. At times the tears are topping the dam just about to break over the top. I restrain them with every bit of courage and strength I can muster.

As time goes by, and with practice, it gets easier. The details become less important to communicate. Getting others on board to help and support me becomes more important than the details. "I was impacted during a re-organization," I tell them. End of story. I engage them on forward events like job search and not backwards. It keeps me focused. I stopped trying to justify.

\* \* \*

Your new story is not simple. It's intertwined with company politics and financial decisions or changes to organizational structures that are seemingly simple to you, but complicated to try and tell. If you try to tell that story in detail, you are going to lose your audience. They will glaze over and before you can take a breath, they will figure out how to move on to another subject. And if they do listen, they probably don't care about the details. People will care more about you, and your situation. They will care about what they might be able to do to help.

Don't be afraid to tell your story. Don't be afraid to network to everyone that you know. For one simple reason. You never know who people are or who they know. The next person around the corner that you meet could lead you to your next job. First, communicate the event. Phrase it briefly and make it a non-event as career placement coaches would have you do. "I was impacted during a re-organization," or "I was impacted when the company downsized." Done. Make the focus the event of job search and what you are looking for.

You need to be able to tell them briefly what it is that you do. For an accountant or sales person, this may be easy. For others the skills and job you are looking for may not be as easy to articulate. Break it down into simple terms and a few short phrases. This is your elevator speech. For those of us that are not comfortable in doing this, then write your elevator speech. Have it in a written memo or notebook in your pocket. Look at it and practice it. But practice it with live candidates.

UnChosen

The more you deliver the speech the better you will be at it. Repetition is the key to selling and to getting your best message across to your audience. You have to sell yourself, because no one else will. Few will care deeply about you and have a high level of interest in your future other than your immediate family. Remove all embarrassment, remove the doubt. Just do it and go for it. Be relentless. Never stop doing this. Even after you have found your job. The job hunt should never end.

Everyone needs an elevator speech. No matter what you are trying to sell. Especially when trying to sell yourself, you need an elevator speech. You need a way to communicate your message clearly, in a very short amount of time. Most will tell you that your elevator speech needs to be 30 seconds, but you really need to keep it in the 10 to 15 second range, and make it compelling enough that you will get questions and they will want to know more. You need to practice it out loud until you can say it in your sleep. It needs to sound natural and unrehearsed.

### Peter & the Elevator Speech

A key sales technique is to have an elevator speech. This is what you rehearse to tell the CEO, or a person that has little time on why they should listen to you.

You may have 15 seconds or 15 minutes. It will vary with every situation. I pride myself in the elevator speech. The theory is that if you can simplify your pitch into a short message it will have the best effect. Professional sales people practice their elevator speech and have ready and refine it each day. Every time you make the elevator pitch it gets better. Mine to this day goes something like this. "I'm an international sales and business professional and my specialty is to open and penetrate new markets or introduce new products globally." In general networking and telling people that may be friends or acquaintances, it goes something like this; "My role now with companies is to take them from one point to the next. I work on a contract or as a consultant and then exit the company. The expertise that I bring is international market expansion and growth in technology products or services. If you happen to hear of any company looking for someone with my skills please let me know." At this point I always have a business card handy. To this day this is my elevator speech. As I continue to network each day and I devote time one or two hours per week to network with social media. I also constantly reach out to friends, congratulate them on new roles or network for my friends who need assistance or are unemployed. Once I land my new opportunity, I'm positioning myself and looking for the next opportunity.

\* \* \*

The elevator speech is your ticket to networking and getting referrals to opportunities. It's the ticket to telling your story. Practicing the elevator speech until you are comfortable is your ticket to overcoming the fear of engaging other people with your story.

## Chapter 11

## This Hell We Call Job Search

It's bad enough that you are on the trauma train. As the train has now traveled down the tracks riding the hills, curves, and valleys of the emotional trauma experience, you've now accelerated into a rollercoaster ride. It's called Job Search. Or, as we affectionately call it, 'hell.' Because it is…a living hell. Gradual and sharp turns wait for you up ahead. You'll climb to the peaks and plunge into the valleys. You will creep up slow grades as your confidence builds reaching a point of what you think will be a glorious end to the ride, then drop off an unseen peak into darkness. There is no greater or more terrible ride. And unlike most rollercoasters where the ride feels short, this one will feel like it is never going to end.

The baggage you carried onto this ride is heavy. Self-doubt, depression, financial obligations and challenges, stress, fear, uncertainty, and self-doubt. Yes, you screwed up and packed self-doubt twice.

This ride knows and shows no favoritism. It is blind. It has no prejudice. It treats everyone the same. Job search is the greatest of the challenges you face in the UnChosen world. It is the hardest and most trying part of the journey.

## UnChosen

Job search is a juggling act of many components. Completing your resume, searching job postings, filling out applications, making phone calls, developing connections, networking, interviewing, and following up. And while UnChosen, emotions are running high. It's like juggling on a high wire, or better yet, on a rollercoaster.

The idea of the job search seems quite simple. Find a job posting that matches your skills, apply, interview, get hired, and start work. Seems simple enough. Unfortunately, it's a complex system of pieces, parts and challenges to navigate and overcome.

Not so many decades ago it was simpler. Maybe not easier, but simpler. You picked up the local newspaper and scoured through the job postings. You dropped by to put in an application in person, or you mailed in your resume. The world was smaller, less global. In those days contacts were easier to make, people easier to get access to. At least it seemed so.

Today, complications of the exponential degree. The computer and internet brought new and immense challenges. Software packages that filter through resumes for key words. Your resume may never reach a real person. Online application forms, some of which take more than an hour to complete, ask for information that will never be used. Some have you create a login for the company site. A world of sophisticated tools and processes, all new barriers to landing that job. It's a system that is broken. There are no standard set of rules, just rough guidelines. The fact is that you are playing a game with loose rules, on a wide playing field, with others on the hiring side that are all running onto the field with their own twisted set of rules.

You are also dealing with an inept system of human resource departments and professionals that are not fully developed in the art or science of hiring; that don't have an established process; and have not organized and coordinated a plan with their hiring managers. Because there is hardly an established process, it will be hard to get closure and confirmation at different points of the process from the application to post interview. There are some organizations that do have processes and manage those processes very well. They are to be commended. Unfortunately, they are the exception and not the rule.

In addition, you're dealing with hiring managers that don't know how to hire. Chances are they have never had any structured training at all, and are loitering through their own ad hoc process and trying to get support from their HR organization. In the end, you're going to find a lot of people that are not sensitive to your situation; will not treat the process with professionalism; and will not do what they commit they are going to do. Many times in your job search you are going to hear "we will follow-up with you or call you back within two weeks." That's a phone call you will never receive.

With that thought, know also that communication in general has changed also. The telephone used to be the primary mode of communication. Then came voicemail where you could leave a message that you hoped might get returned. Then E-mail allowed hiring managers to communicate in a less intimate manner. Some hide behind it. Most times e-mails are exchanged before the first phone call ever occurs, if at all. There seems to be less focus on the person and direct interaction. There is more focus on what is in writing.

This is a broken system with broken tools where some work and some don't. Many companies have migrated to online submission of applications. Input your information, and attach your resume. You will spend a few minutes or more than an hour filling out the application. You may never get any response or any kind. If you do get a response, or even land the job, the chances of all the info being used is slim. Behind that tool where you submitted your application most likely is a search engine, and it's not human. When applicants became too plentiful to be managed easily (or so the story goes), software tools that execute key word searches were engaged to narrow down the field. Many of the same human resource professionals that regularly use these tools today will agree that those key word search tools don't work. If so, then why use them? The bottom line is that going through this method might not even get you to a human. You input your information, you get the incredibly efficient acknowledgement from the system that your application has been received. And now you wait. And you wait. And you wait.

As you search for job postings to submit those applications, you'll find another great problem in the system. There is not a universally accepted set of job descriptions in a glossary somewhere that everyone follows. Senior Manager, Manager, Director, or Vice President might all be the label for the same type role at different companies. There are times you will see job titles that will only mean something internally to the company that is posting it. This makes online searches difficult and frustrating.

The description in the job posting is an additional source of frustration. Some are short and generally vague. Others are incredibly long and include Job duties and requirements in major length and detail. You'll wonder if they could ever find that super human that could successfully perform all those duties and have all those skills. It's hard to discern what capabilities and core competencies are most important to them for the position. Reading through job postings and trying to sort through this mess of requirements to determine what they are really looking for is maddening! Especially when you are emotional and desperate.

So, you sit down to get started. Step 1, write a resume. Simple, right? Wrong. A resume is a continual work in progress. It is also a work in imperfection. It will never be finished, and it will never be perfect. There is no objective measurement or rule you will find to judge it, nor objective person to review and approve it that will make it complete or finished. Each person brings their own perspective and their own subjective view of what it should be. It is the one document that 100 people can read and review and give you 100 different opinions on what will make it better. Take this part out. Put this part in. Change the font. It's too wordy. Not enough content. Wrong content. You will get all the feedback. Some professional resume writers might create pure garbage for you, or destroy what you already have. Good friends that don't know a darn thing about resumes will give feedback. Anyone that has ever had a job, been a manager of people, worked in human resources, been a friend, a neighbor, or a casual acquaintance will have an opinion. Everyone is a critic. There's one on every corner. You could be stalled here forever trying to get this document perfect. It's frustrating beyond belief! Just remember perfection is not achievable.

On another level, trying to cram years of experience on a piece of paper to communicate your skills and abilities seems almost impossible.

## Greg's Struggle to Prepare

After more than 20 years with the same company at my last career stop, I have hardly had to account for what I can do, or how well I can do it. My reputation has preceded itself inside and outside of my peer group. At a very basic level, I'm good at what I do. I know that because I haven't been fired, and my performance evaluations reflect the fact that I know what I'm doing, and I do it pretty darn well.

But now I'm out of work, and having to justify what I do and how I do it. I have to be able to explain to others what it is I do and how good I am at it. The people that are interviewing me have no point of reference. They don't know me, and most likely don't know anyone that knows me. To make matters worse, I will have less than an hour in most cases to convince them of what I am capable of. This is an extremely important point to recognize. For even as I start to write my resume, I am dumbfounded as to how in the world you put skills and abilities on paper where others will read it, and get it. How in the world can they get what you can do from a piece of paper? Let alone figure out how well you can do it.

*　*　*

To make matters worse. Just when you thought they could not get worse. Some recruiters and professionals in the job placement industry will tell you to have two or three resumes for different types of jobs or roles you might apply for. Some will tell you to cater the resume to each job posting, making sure you have included key words from the job posting in the resume. (Remember the key word search machine.) You are in essence trying to beat the system. It's a type of reverse engineering. You will spend hours, days, and weeks trying to beat the system and working on the resume trying to get that document 'finished.'

<u>Greg's Resume</u>

I began working with a job placement service as a perk included in my severance package. It indeed was a perk because I was a sponge ready to learn everything possible about this new world I had been thrown into. I wanted to get good at job search, and quickly. My personal coach taught me about all the balls that were going to have to be juggled. One of them was the resume.

I labored hard and as I was beginning to realize how hard it is to put twenty plus years of successful career on TWO pages, I also began to be frustrated as I began to get the critics on every corner telling me how to "fix" it. I was also spending an incredible amount of time in the beginning trying to play the three resume game.

As I was applying for jobs, I was beginning to feel like Sybil. I had identity crisis. Just keeping track of what resume was e-mailed to which person, and attached to which application became a job in itself.

As I sat in my home office one day trying to resolve this problem I was just about to scream. I just wanted to get it done so I could move on to the next important thing…getting the damn job.

I set up a call with my personal career coach. After an emotional discussion with her, I resolved to one version that she helped create. It represented my skills, work history, and my brand. It followed all generally accepted rules including format.

After my decision that this was the resume, it was like a great weight from stress was lifted.

* * *

There will always be something else to improve upon in the resume. The best you can do is to follow industry standards, and make sure that your brand is right. The best you can feel is that it represents your brand, and represents you well; who you are, and what you can do.

Peter's Resume Strategy

A resume is simply a document that tells a story, but not the entire story. So, how in the heck can I get the resume to tell my story? After spending money with consultants and laboring long and hard, I finally came to the conclusion that it is not the resume that tells the story. I have tried having resumes for various positions or even industries. I finally settled on one professional resume that tells a story that is truthful and not exaggerated.

What really tells the whole story, my story, is me. I realized that I have to get in front of someone to interview. I do well in face to face meetings, I'm a sales professional and consider myself a good closer. I had to ditch the resume as the primary story and realize it was not the answer. The probability of getting your resume read by anyone that does not know you is very low. I rely on networking and getting a meeting with someone that either knows me or with someone that I have been recommended and introduced to. A lunch meeting with someone goes much further than emailing resumes from job search web sites. My resume only acts as a supporting document. I finally decided to ditch all the job search social media and recruiters. I get the in person meeting, and use the resume for support.

\* \* \*

After you have mastered the perpetually imperfect resume, you'll next land an interview. Your emotions sour. Now you have a solid opportunity to land a job. Let the emotional and self-esteem beatings begin.

You now have a chance to advocate for yourself, something you have been told all your life not to do. "Don't brag on yourself." You've most likely heard this all through childhood. So, unless you might be a sales person by nature, this process does not come naturally to you. Outside of the emotional and stressful state you are in advocating for yourself would be difficult enough. Add all the emotions you are carrying around in your head and your heart. At times interviewing feels like an interrogation. You never really had to justify your existence before, but some interviewers are going to make you feel like you are having to do so now. There you will sit, feeling desperate, already emotionally beaten, and now in front of this other person that is making this process about as uncomfortable as it could ever be. Part of you wants to get up and walk out, but you can't. You can't afford to.

The next interview may be a totally different experience. Your interviewer may be personable, compassionate, and upbeat. This situation may be just as bad emotionally. You will leave that interview on a great high. You're feeling good. Everything went *so* well. They were *so* positive. They made you feel good about yourself. They talked about benefits, company culture, how you would fit in, what your work life would be like, and how great the company is. They sold you, and you are ready to buy. You are sure you got the position, or at least you will move to the next step. Only to be shot down with a rejection e-mail, or worse you never hear from them again.

Interviewing is something that no one ever wants to be good at. If job search is Hell then interviewing is the Devil. It's the toughest part of the job search journey. You're continually preparing for a test that has no study guide. The question pool is endless. Whether the answers are correct or not is at the discretion of the interviewer. It's purely subjective.

Every single interview you do will be different. Every interviewer is different. One of the most astounding things that has happened, is the unprofessional nature of the interviewers these days. For those that remember that a coat and tie is a must for every interview, will be shocked to find the state of affairs of the dress code these days. Popular convention still dictates that the interviewee should wear a coat and tie, preferably a suit. Most generations, with the exception of maybe the millennials, have been brought up to dress professionally for the interview. As a candidate showing up to an interview, it's disheartening to see that interviewers don't follow the convention. You will sit in many interviews and wonder if the hiring manager is actually taking this seriously. Not only are they not wearing a tie, they most likely might be in jeans, tennis shoes, and a golf shirt. All the while *you* are serious. You are in a suit and ready for business. You need a job. You need a new career. Your life and well-being depends upon this process. It is depending on them.

Interviewing is the greatest emotional drain of all in the job search process. Your interviewer, or interviewers take you through this test, this journey. All the while they are pumping you up or tearing you down. If they have pumped you up,

## UnChosen

you feel like someone with that big fish on the line. You know you got it. It's there in the water somewhere. Just now, how the heck do you get it in the boat. You've answered all the questions. Talked about the position and the company, and they have made you feel like you could start tomorrow. You walk out the door on a new high, telling yourself this story in your head about how you got it. You felt good about it. They were smiling, seemingly impressed. They even used language about how you could really fit into the organization and be successful in the role. How could they not hire you?

### Greg's Interview Coaster

I received a great connection to a potential job through a friend at church. The connection called me and we spoke initially on the phone. What I thought would be a very short conversation turned into more than an hour of dialog sharing vision and experience. We hit it off quickly and set up a follow-up lunch.

I arrived at lunch that day, prepared, and excited. Excited to continue the robust conversation that would lead to opportunity and employment.

Lunch was incredible. I ate very little, and talked a lot. It could not have gone better. She was absorbing my every word and we were connecting on values, strategy, and people management. By the end of over and hour of conversation, she was beginning to talk about how to get me in the door with her company. She indicated at one point that she would love to just take me back with her and put me on the job that day. Emotions were running high, and I was pumped up! I left her that day feeling on top of the world and sure that a job was in my future.

Time passed. She finally reached out to set up a formal "interview." That interview day was strange. She and I spoke briefly, then she put me in a room to interview with what would be my peers. These were people that in our previous conversations she had clearly shown no confidence in. I spoke with them for an hour or more. It was clear why I was so badly needed in the organization. They were not leaders. They were not forward thinking. After interviewing with them, she and I spoke briefly again before I departed. We spoke about the team again, and the challenges. I left still very confident.

Time passed again. Lots of time. She went silent and dark and there was no communication of any kind for weeks. Finally, on a Friday evening, an e-mail. Not a phone call. Just an e-mail.

## UnChosen

At this point I had been on the street for more than 15 months. I was in a bad state of mind during that time. Most days at the house we were like a family mourning the death of a loved one. We didn't want to acknowledge unemployment. No, I didn't want to acknowledge it. My wife was unsure when and how to engage me about it. Every time she asked me about an opportunity, a connection, or a job interview or follow-up, it was a reminder that I was unemployed. To me it was a reminder that I was a failure.

As I was interviewing with this lady for this great opportunity, I was on a high, encouraged, and positive!

Now the e-mail. She had decided not to extend me the opportunity. Devastated. I remember vividly as I was watching a music concert with my son. As I looked at the e-mail, I cried!!! She didn't even have the guts or professional courtesy to give me a call. She was a coward, and I was an emotional mess.

\* \* \*

As you have departed the interview, one of the last questions you ask (or you should have asked) is "What are the next steps?" You will hear about their process; about other candidates; about what the next interview might involve; or schedules that need to be worked out. Most of the time you will be told that someone will be getting back to you within a couple weeks. It's the biggest lie ever told, and most frequently told, by hiring managers. It may be told with the best of intentions, but told without resolve or commitment. It's just a great big lie. You leave the interview with a good feeling, possibly an emotional high. This confidence in self and positive emotions begin to deteriorate as time passes once the interview is over.

### Greg's Phone Never Rings

I interviewed for a position and everything went very well. I felt at many times during the interview that I might be driving the conversation a little too much, but felt it went well. I could tell neither the hiring manager nor the HR representative were very good at interviewing. First interview landed me a final interview that would be composed of a four hour exercise. I was to take a problem, involve the right department heads, ask questions, develop a plan, and propose a solution. Four hours.

At the end of the presentation, we spoke briefly again. Me, the hiring manager, and the HR representative. I was told I had missed a couple things, but had done well considering I was an outsider to the company and the industry. It was a Thursday just after noon as we were finishing up. The hiring manager told me at this point that he had received all the executive approvals needed for the position, and just needed final approval from his manager. He indicated that the latest I would hear from him would be the very next Wednesday. He said it might be Monday, or as early as Friday, the next day. But he was adamant that it would definitely be by Wednesday of the next week.

Years later, I am still waiting for that phone call...

\* \* \*

Hope. All UnChosen people carry it around. Without hope there is nothing. But hope leaves us exposed emotionally. Ready for the picking. Ready for the fall.

Not surprisingly, many interviews are done by phone these days or by Skype or other video capable internet applications. All these different situations have their own advantages and disadvantages. Phone interviews allow you to have notes in front of you, but give you (and the interviewer) no opportunity to read body language and facial expressions. Video interviews give you part of the visual, but not all of it, and they introduce a risk of bad connection affecting your experience.

One of the most important parts of job search is making connections. Introductions and referrals are the most productive part of the process. Career placement professionals and recruiters will quote studies that show that somewhere between 60 and 80 percent of jobs are found through a personal connection and not through the hiring process of putting in an application, interviewing, etc. Then why play this game with processes and applications and red tape? Regulatory rules and laws dictate that employers be fair and consistent providing the same opportunity for all.

So here you go. Filling out applications, e-mailing resumes, making phone calls, interviewing, and following up. It's a grueling and frustrating process. Searching for a job is in a way masochism. It's like getting up every day and taking a beating on the inside. It's hitting things head on that you know are going to hurt. A continual beating; daily, weekly, monthly. Opportunities that never turn into a phone call. Phone calls that never turn into interviews. Interviews that never turn into return phone calls, or jobs. Interviews that never result in anything, not even an e-mail. A job opportunity on the hook, then the line breaks.

Such is job search. At times the rise and fall of emotions takes a long period of time. Sometimes it is short and fleeting.

UnChosen

It may only last a day, or just hours. Having an opportunity provides hope. Hope of any kind is good; and it's bad. Hope will bring you up to a high. But hope hinged on an opportunity is your emotions just primed for the fall. The longer you go through the process, the more your emotions swing lower and your confidence is chipped away.

The job search hell requires discipline, tenacity, and faith in yourself and your abilities to make it through and survive. It requires the same strategy as talking to people; practice, practice, practice. The great thing about it is, once you have done the work and prepared yourself, it's just like riding a bicycle. Once you learn how to put all the pieces together it becomes second nature. No one ever really wants to be good at job search. They want to land a job and just work, plan your life, and live. The reality is the new work place does not allow us that luxury. "The Social Contract" was cancelled. We live under new rules. The up side is as we keep ourselves ready it keeps us fresh and relevant.

Knowing how to find the next job provides its own level of mental and emotional comfort and security. It provides a mechanism to feel more in control of your life and your career.

### Peter – Every Day is a New Day

The interview and networking process can be brutal

for anyone, including a seasoned sales professional like me. The constant discussions and follow ups that lead to nothing. Each day is disappointment when there is no positive news to tell your family or spouse. What works for me is just to put a close to the day. Focus on the positive with the family. Enjoy a good meal and exercise. That was key in keeping myself positive. The next day is a new day. I would take it one day at a time. Once the day was over, I would review what lessons I learned and forget that day. Move on to the next day and focus on the job at hand; searching for a job.

* * *

# Part 3

# Recovery

# Recovering Emotionally, Physically, and Financially.

## Chapter 12

## Healing and Becoming Whole Again

Landing a new job will have little to do with your complete recovery. It will be the beginning, but not the single occurrence that will heal you. Getting a job does not necessarily mean that you have recovered. Let's say that again so we all understand it. You may even want to read this out loud to yourself: *getting rehired does not necessarily mean you will be whole again and be healed.*

<u>Greg Goes Back to Work</u>

Finally, after 18 months, there is big relief in getting a job. Financially it means some stability and the ability to relax somewhat and take a breath.

I'm in my first week of work and I feel like a fish out of water. It's uncomfortable. I mean *really* uncomfortable. This is not the work I'm used to, nor the people I am used to working with. I am in a strange land with strange and different people.

I'm going through orientation, and I feel unimportant, unproductive, and really uncomfortable. What the heck am I doing here? And why can't I go back to the days of the past?

I wake up occasionally thinking it was all a dream and that I will be at my old job with all the familiar people. Then I snap out of it and reality sets in again.

I also have a feeling every day that it could not work out, and I would be on the street again. I have no confidence in myself and my abilities. Be UnChosen whittled away at my confidence. Days, weeks, and months of not landing a job continue the mental erosion of my confidence level. When will all this be over?

I have always loved working, but now for the first time in my life I'm wishing that I was done with all this non-sense and could just retire.

After being unemployed for so long, I'm not even sure what normal is anymore. I keep longing for that feeling that I had before. That feeling of belonging. The feeling of confidence in my abilities and what I do on a day to day basis. I long for the days when it wasn't necessarily routine, but I knew day to day and in the weeks to come what I had in front of me, and a confidence to get it done. I felt secure in my job, and could plan my future social activities, work activities, holidays, and vacations. I could plan financially weeks, months, and years in advance.

Routine, I just need routine. I long for it, and want for it. It is at the very center of my being and at the forefront of my thoughts. Normal, I just want to feel normal. Weeks and months have gone by and the new life I have does not feel normal yet. I'm not sure it ever will. I wake up some days and hope that it was all a nightmare, and when I get out of bed I will get ready for work and go back to my old job, just like it was before. I'll pick up with my work family, just where we left off. Those days are gone and are never coming back. I know it now. I know it, but there is still a small part of me that continues to stay in denial.

\* \* \*

We are creatures of habit and when our routine is upset, we are uncomfortable. Without "The Social Contract," there are no guarantees of routine, of planning your career from one end to the other within the same company. This is the new normal. 'Routine' and 'comfortable' will never be the same again. UnChosen is either in your past, or it will most likely be in your future.

It's a hard message to deliver to others that going through this journey and all the inner and outer trials that in the end, a

## UnChosen

job is probably not going to make you healthy again. It's a difficult realization to assimilate in your brain.

### Healing & Recovering

So, how do we heal and find our new normal? Studies show that it is easier for someone to recover from the loss of a spouse than it is to recover from layoff or long time unemployment. What is a long time? The definition will vary from individual to individual and is based on a lot of factors. How long have you worked for that company or been in that role? How financially stretched are you? Existence of monetary resources makes a longer span of time more bearable than someone that has none. Those that have created a life dependent upon living paycheck to paycheck will suffer immediately. Here are some important things to do, know, and plan around as you begin your road to recovery.

### Let Go!

Life now has become a complicated struggle to survive. If you have severance from being UnChosen, then you can plan your life somewhat. But for those that don't have any severance and bills keep rolling in, life is getting very difficult. This is where family relationships are tested and sometimes severely. You and your partner along with family truly have to start cutting costs. Putting up houses for sale. Selling cars. Getting kids out of private schools. Getting in more debt. Working a second job to catch up, or an entry level job just for the income to put some food on the table during the transition.

Keep this in mind. Do what you must do to survive. Material things will come and go in life. Let them go. Survive. Don't fight it. Survive and get through with those things that are most important to you in your value system. If material things are at the top of your value system, you will need to take a hard look at your life and that value system. Things may not survive, but *you* can!

Another opportunity will show itself and those material things will return. This is all a part of the ride on the emotional roller coaster. Live and choose survival. Don't let materiality get you down. Forget the past and live for the now. Prepare for a brighter future.

Focus on The Future

If you don't know where you are going you are never going to get there. You also are never going to make any progress mired in the quicksand of your situation today. It is imperative to continue to focus on your future state. That doesn't mean that you need to visualize 5 years from now.

## UnChosen

Although thinking long term is not a bad idea. But during this time of job loss it's important to focus on short term goals and things that will move you forward to recovery. Financially you may need to make major lifestyle adjustments, or at least understand what your benchmark in time will be to have to make those hard decisions.

Meet at least once a week with your support person. Set goals of completing job applications or setting up networking meetings. Every step forward is a step closer to your recovery. Think forward, not backward. Think in a new framework, not in the framework of the life you lived before.

### Keep Physically Fit

As you age it is especially important to keep fit. As you are mentally drained it is important to keep fit. As you look for your next career stop, it is important to keep fit. Think about who you would rather hire. Someone fit and healthy looking, or someone out of shape given both have the same job skills. Keeping your body active and fit also keeps your mind active and fit. Take time for some type of workout at least a couple of days a week. It will keep you sharper and more focused. Feeling good physically lends to a better mental state. Exercise time also gives your mind a rest.

Walk, run, or workout with weights. Believe it or not,

physical exhaustion will help you rest, which will help you mentally rest and be in a better mental state. Physical exhaustion can create a breakthrough that will be a catalyst for a mental breakthrough. Physical exhaustion will help create a better resting state in which your body will rest. When your body can rest, your mind will follow.

### Focus on Your Strengths

One of the worst parts of being laid off is the feeling of worthlessness. That feeling that you didn't so something right, or that you didn't do it well enough to stay in your job. Then after a time you begin to question your skills and abilities. There is an enormous amount of self-doubt. What was it really that you did and how well did you do it?

This is the point in time when it is important that you are able to sit down and define what your hard and soft skills are and see them in the perspective of a job. Define your talent in abilities, not to a specific job or job title. Remember back to the things that made you successful in previous roles.

Here's an example. What if you were a Business Analyst and you are UnChosen. You continue to look, but not many business analyst positions are available. You need a paradigm shift in thinking. Think about what your skill sets are, not what your job function was. Pick the top three things that you really do well. For a business analyst, that might be that you are very well organized, you are great with numbers, and you understand business processes. Now, as you look at job postings and descriptions, you can begin to map those skill sets to other positions with similar needs. So, when people ask you what you do, you don't say you are a business analyst, you say you are a highly focused business professional with strong organizational skills, a key understanding of business processes, and able to work intricately with financial information.

Know your strengths but know them in terms of skills, abilities, and competencies.

## A Support Group

It is nearly impossible to get through being UnChosen without a supportive family and/or a strong bond with some supportive friends. At this point it is extremely important to surround yourself with positive people. If you have people that are encouraging your bitterness toward the company, the situation, or life in general, you need to get away from them and limit the amount of time you spend with them. Or, better yet, tell them out right that you do not really care to harp on the past. Tell them you are more interested in figuring out the future and focusing on the road ahead. Surround yourself with people who know your strengths and will remind you often that you have skills and abilities that are valuable.

Family is where it will start. Their love and compassion is the foundation that you will build your recovery on. They are in this with you, and as much as you are struggling, you need to remember that they are struggling too. They are going to feel helpless. They need to understand how valuable their support is.

Good friends. Let's go as far as to say one single good friend. A good friend is key. This may even be a family member. But this needs to be a person that you share your deepest fears and feelings with. It's like your own personal therapist. Okay, they ARE your therapist. Find this person and schedule regular time with them. Remember you should be careful not to just take them the pain and suffering. Remember to share the successes with them too. They are not going to hang around if all you do is bring them down.

### Peter, Friends & Therapy

> I spend a lot of time alone and away from my family and trusted friends. For 25 years, I traveled the globe to over 82 countries. I have spent a lot of time in hotels traveling and eating alone at restaurants. I have spent several Christmas holidays away from family.

The pain and the ability to deal with loneliness is a skill that needs to be refined. But the loneliness from being "UnChosen" is different from travel loneliness. The loneliness is really bad and I'm the most outgoing guy in the world. It's lonely because it has finally sunk in that all your so-called colleagues don't care. They don't call you, they don't help you, and they are doing just fine without you.

You need a mentor, coach, or just a friend that will listen. You really need an experienced professional that has gone through this before. The search for a mentor is the key. This is the person that will help you get your emotions intact. Face it, you are screwed up now and you need help. I didn't know how much I needed a mentor and it took me a long time to find one. Only after the third company following the dream job exit did I find my mentor. So, I had to learn it all the hard way. I had no coach, no help, nobody to listen to me. Keeping up a positive spirit was difficult and I'm a very positive person. My psychosomatic health was at risk. I couldn't sleep, lost weight, and that was not the worst. I found myself delving into self-pity and blaming others for my plight in life and negativity. I found a personal coach that was a positive impetus needed to overcome the negative.

\* \* \*

A support group or a one good friend is key. Beyond that, if you can afford it or you can network to someone that can work with you on trade or pro-bono basis, find a career coach or a personal coach. If possible, find this person before you are really forced into needing them.

<u>A Journal</u>

If you do not have a journal. Go buy one today. Some of you are going to ask, "What's a journal?" Sometimes called a diary, but a journal is much more than that. A diary is just a few scribbled lines of what happened to you that day. A journal is a chronicle of what's happening to you emotionally at a point in time. It's a personal recording of your life. Almost as good, and sometimes even better than having a close friend to talk to is having a journal. Writing out your true thoughts and feelings, if even to yourself, is absolutely invaluable.

The ability to sit down and articulate your thoughts and feelings, especially those that you are not comfortable telling someone else, is unbelievably therapeutic. It may be the best therapy you can get. It allows you to work things out, and it will be a reference for you as you recover. You should never

UnChosen

forget these fears and self-doubt you are having. It is a record of your growth through this troubled time and your personal growth in life. You should journal in good times and bad.

Come to Peace

Yep, you read that correctly. You are going to have to. No matter how you exited your company and felt initially about your dismissal, you need closure. You have to realize that this was not personal. No. Forget that! It was personal. But it was only personal to you. For the company it was an objective, financial, and business decision. Remember, decisions are made with the health of the business first. You are at best in second position for their decisions. You were in second position at best when you were UnChosen. You will have to come to grips with that.

Know that you and your life are larger than that job and your time with that company. Write the person that let you go a letter. You don't even have to mail it to them. Burn it or throw it away. Better yet, write in your journal what you would write to them. If that does not work, figure out another way, but let it go.

Faith

Have faith. To begin with, have faith in yourself. Know

that you are going to get to a better place, and that you are going to be the person most responsible for your growth and success. Have faith in your abilities. Have faith that you will have the strength to weather this storm. You are going to fall down. There are going to be days when you feel you are never going to recover. Allow yourself a little mourning, but not much. Pick yourself up and move on.

Then have faith and believe that this path is bringing you to a better place. That place may not be a high paying job, and you need to be resolved to that. That place you find, may be a stronger bond with your family. It may be a closer look at, and bond with your value system. It may be a closer walk with God and life. Whatever that better place is, you need to look for it and realize it will probably come in a form that you may not expect. Just have faith that this is where you are headed.

### Keep Positive

Closely following behind faith in yourself should be daily coaching to keep your spirits up and to stay positive. Fear will try to creep in. Don't let it! One of the hardest things to do on a continuing basis is to coach yourself into a positive attitude.

### Peter's Fear of the Present & Future

Fear will set in. Fear of the unknown. This will vary

from person to person depending on your personality. In my case I deal with fear well and will dive off into the swimming pool without looking. My experience in the Middle East and geo-politics have formed my psyche to respect fear and to harness it to gain strength. Man has three innate fears; fear of close spaces, fear of heights, and fear of failure. The fear of failure is innate in us to protect us from harming ourselves. It's the survival of the species. Loneliness and fear work hand in hand. They are the work of the dark side and will paralyze your mind if you let it overcome you.

While residing in Pakistan and working with a European multinational firm, we came across a group of militants one evening who were robbing cars, assaulting women, and taking small children for human trafficking. We came under fire and our security returned their fire luckily with superior weaponry, quickly and efficiently. We survived that evening and four other similar events. Fear of death and fear of being captured, tortured or having your head chopped off on a YouTube video: this is the way that fear works as your ally. But, it will work as your enemy too. It can kill you just like the enemy can kill you. We have all gone through some form of formal or informal training in our lives. Remember your training. Never, never give up. Respect fear but don't let it overwhelm your thoughts.

\* \* \*

There's lots of things to be afraid of. There are lots of reasons to be afraid. There a lot of things you could focus on and be negative about. You also have a lot of things to be thankful for. There are a lot of things going 'right' if you just look for them. Focus on the positive. Keep your mind off the negative. The negative will kill you and will overcome your mind, soul, and body. It is like cancer and you may not see it coming. You may not even know that you have it.

## Analyze Your Life Holistically

One of the more important things to realize during this tough time is that this is just *a point in time* in your life and does not define your entire existence. This is not an easy thing to do. Today is relevant and when things are not going well it's hard to think about anything but this. The pain is real and it's not easy to look beyond it. After a considerable amount of time you may even begin to wonder if you will ever work again. Visualizing returning to normal becomes very difficult.

Perspective is hard to come by. Look at life holistically. Look back and remember some hard times and how you pulled through them. Or take a look at others you know that went through hard times. Talk to them. Understand they made it. You can too.

### A Plan

You need a plan. A financial plan, a social plan, a job search plan.

At first, you just need to learn to take baby steps. If you try to eat this entire elephant at the first sitting, you will fail. Set yourself some small goals. In the first few days evaluate your financial situation, make some lists of people to start talking to, and set up a schedule for yourself. Schedule job search preparation and activity time. Schedule time to exercise. Schedule time with your best friend or support person.

Here's what *not* to do. Don't start putting in applications for jobs or setting up interviews. You are in no mental state to be talking to prospective hiring managers. You are going to be frantic and scared and they are going to know it. Regroup and gather your life and emotions together first. Even if you were already prepared for this event in your life or have been through it before; stand down. Pause. Plan and organize first.

Baby steps. Get a plan together. Recruit those that you will need to help you get through. Walk at first. Don't try to run.

## Own It!

The most important piece to the puzzle is the realization that your life and career are yours and no one else is responsible. You should never leave your career to a company or another individual to manage and hold. You have to own it. There is a great quote from Jim Rohn, "No one can do your pushups for you!" No one can own your career but you. No one *should* own your career but you!

## Peter's Revelation

It took a lot of pain and riding the emotional roller coaster before I realized that my recovery starts with me. I was the one in charge of my life. I had found my first career so I had to continue finding my next career. Once this revelation had become clear I was on the road to actually getting results.

I awoke each morning with a clear objective. Find my next career. It was my job to find a job. It was entirely up to me and only up to me. Everything else that was a distraction was noise. I trained myself to ignore the noise. Putting on my earphones to drown out the sound and listen only to sweet music of my choosing. Listening only to the positive influences. The friends, relatives or business connections that added value.

Recovery is about the practice of the visualizing, dreaming, and thinking positive and not dwelling on the negative. Once you have arrived in the positive people see you in an optimistic light. Trust me, when you are negative people see you that way. It's hard to hide your body language and what permeates from your emotions. A positive spirit prevails and shows through your personality. Once you are in recovery you are there. You will land the opportunity. You will make it to the next level. The world may still be crashing and burning around you. The difference is that you take no notice. You are in a zone moving in a positive direction at light speed. Nothing gets in your way. You have arrived emotionally.

* * *

The raw truth is that if you leave it up to companies and managers, they will use you for their purposes. Once that use has run its course, you will be left standing on your own.

## Peter Says "Own It!"

I spent a lot of time thinking of "why?" Why did this happen to me? I finally learned after much tribulation that the "why" doesn't matter. There really was no answer to the why I was UnChosen. It just happened to me and to all the thousands of other people that are UnChosen each day from a corporation. The key is what I am going to do next. Am I going to take my destiny in my own hands? Or am I going to sit around and wonder "Why" did this happen to me? As Admiral Farragut said, "Damn the torpedoes and full speed ahead." That's the conclusion that I came to. In fact, revenge and "I'll show you what a good job I can get" set into my psyche.

*  *  *

This is not meant to be delivered in a cynical or obtuse manner. It's a simple fact. As business owners ourselves, we understand that business is created to make money for the owner, owners, or stockholders. If that can't occur, the business is no longer viable. The simple raw truth is that the health of the company *has* to come first in order to serve its employees. The employee must understand that a company will *never* make a decision that will have the health and benefit of the employees in mind first. There is no easy or kind way to deliver that message. But let's repeat it just so we are all clear: A company will *never* make a strategic or tactical decision that will have the best interest of the employees in mind! Employee well-being will always be secondary at best to operating the company.

Knowing that simple fact puts career ownership fully in the hands of *you*, the employee.

## Peter Gets It

My longtime friend George, who was my agent in Greece, provided good advice. He encouraged me to start looking for new industries that are growing. He told me that textiles were over and that Greece was going through a recession. In fact, textiles in Europe had the same fate as North America. George commented that he was expanding his business into the Middle East and trying to get out of the market in Greece. His days were numbered too and he was firing himself. This valuable lesson of firing yourself and being aware of your industry trends was valuable advice. I have used this lesson until this day. I would select companies that are trending upwards, growing and have not reached their maturity. I had ridden the textile industry past maturity and into decline. I would learn to exit on my own terms. I would fire myself when it was time. I would not ride the same horse for too long. I would never be loyal to any corporation after that point. I was on my road to being a private corporate mercenary.

\* \* \*

There is a saying—"When one door closes, another one opens." Many people will tell you this during this time of transition you are in. Open your own doors. Close others behind you when it's time for you to move on.

## Chapter 13

## Chosen Again

Being UnChosen made you feel alone. You realize now you were not alone. You know now that others have taken this trip and had the same feelings and experiences. You know now that others that have been UnChosen are carrying the same burdens and emotional trauma behind a silent, stoic mask. Everything that has happened to you is all very real. What you felt is normal. All that you carried inside you has been carried silently by others.

Being UnChosen made you feel afraid. Afraid of running out of money, of failure, and of the future and unknowns ahead. You now know that everything heals in time. You know that this event in your life is just an event. A point in time. It is something that will pass and it is something you can conquer. Your fear is quailed by your ability to learn and adapt.

Being UnChosen made you feel lost and out of control. You were in unknown territory, and felt no control of yourself and your destiny. Life whirled around you as situations and experiences came at you at an incredible pace. Your head was spinning. You traveled on the trauma train, and rode on the emotional rollercoaster all the while feeling like you were not at the controls. You wanted to jump off, slow it down, or just make it stop! But you didn't know how to make that happen. You've never been on this kind of ride before.

You made the journey and finally the vehicle came to a stop. You reached the destination, but the destination you reached was not just a new job. Your destination is bigger and greater than that. The journey ended with being Chosen again. Chosen again not by a hiring manager or a company. You have Chosen yourself.

All this time, while riding the emotional rollercoaster and the trauma train, you never realized you had the power. But you had to go through the experiences to realize it. It's like Dorothy at the end of *The Wizard of Oz* as she finds out that the power has always been within her. Dorothy is now in control of her destiny, as you are in control of yours.

You have to take charge of yourself, your life, and your career completely. You have to take charge of your mind and your emotions. You might be laid off again, but you will not be UnChosen again. We do not pretend to tell you that being laid off a second time will not be an emotional experience. It will, but this time you will be aware, and in charge of your emotions and your life. You will be prepared.

Each of the encounters on the ride gave you knowledge

and experience needed to toughen your mind, body, and soul. Each encounter and experience made you stronger. You have come out on the other side smarter, tougher, and in control.

The workplace in America has changed. The Social Contract has been canceled. A career no longer looks the same as it used to. There is no expectation of a 'lifelong' engagement with a company. You go to work with a different mindset than yesterday. You now have greater ownership in your career and destiny than ever before. Before you were a tenderfoot stumbling through the woods with no idea how to know what is ahead, what to be afraid of, or how to prepare for it. Today you are prepared and in charge. You have adapted to the new workplace.

### Peter Comes Full Circle

The greatest lesson that I have learned from being UnChosen is the change in my personal attitude to be in charge of my career. No one else will take care of my career or well-being. No corporation or employer will. I have been a solid and top 10 performer producing millions of dollars of revenue for corporations, protecting jobs and adding value to shareholders. That performance provided no guarantee on my career and whether that company would keep me. I have learned to be free, and yes, admittedly more selfish. I now choose who I want to work with, under what conditions, and I exit on my terms. I have become stronger through this process. I am a better business professional and have learned to sell my skills better.

\* \* \*

## Greg Comes Full Circle

When I first began my discussions with my career coach as I exited Coca-Cola she said something very strange and foreign to me. She said "when you land a job that is when you start looking for the next one." At first I was appalled, if not angry. How could that be? I am going to go through all this work and these trials and tribulations to land a job only to turn around and start the process over again? I was taking her only in a literal sense. I also was framing my thoughts with the understanding that "The Social Contract" still existed between companies and employees. I was still under the impression that there was a strong level of loyalty between the two.

What she meant was deeper than that. Only now that I have traveled this journey do I understand fully what she meant. What she really meant is that I should not become stagnant and rely upon the company to do my career planning for me and keep me ready for the next step or the next level in my personal or professional growth. What that statement means is that I should always be networking. I should always be looking for opportunities. I should always be ready with a resume and an elevator speech that articulates what I can do and what kind of opportunities I am looking for. I fully understand now what she was trying to tell me then.

Some of the emotions are still there and they will always be a part of who I am now. But I am resilient and stronger because of them. And now, I am always ready, looking for the next opportunity, the next job. I am not stagnant and rigid. I am flexible, adaptable, and agile.

\* \* \*

It's a paradigm shift in your thinking. It's contradictory to career framework you have been living by for decades. The Social Contract embedded a thought process in your head and heart that you now have to change.

Going to work will be different. Your work will be important, but not singular and primary. You will also have created activities and joined clubs and professional organizations outside of work. You will be a part of a team at work, but that team will not be singular and primary. You will have made friends and built support groups and networks outside of your work group. Your work and what you do is no longer primary to your identity. Your team and your work will not be primary to who you are. It will not be primary to your identity.

This may be a new and different concept to digest. Does this mean that you just view your job as just a job? Does it mean that you don't give 110% every day? No. It doesn't. The passion that you take to work with you and your work ethic should not change. You should work and do your best to help the company be successful. You might be there a year, five years, ten years, or if lucky (and if you decide to), your life time. The difference is now that you are in charge of your career. You are not 'waiting' on the next promotion or opportunity, or for the company to train you.

You are not counting on the company to "take care of you." You will take care of yourself. You also now know that the workplace has changed, and what you should expect from your employer and more importantly yourself has changed. You will always have your resume up to date and ready. You will always be connecting and talking to people. You will

## UnChosen

always be developing yourself. You will keep your interviewing and job search skills sharp. You will always keep yourself in a good and sound financial position. You will always be in control.

Actor Will Smith said it best in an interview — "If you stay ready, you ain't gotta get ready!"

Choose yourself, stay ready, and be in control!

## Epilogue

## The UnChosen Experience Can Happen In Many Ways

We have primarily focused on the UnChosen experience of the employee that has worked for one company for a long time and suddenly laid off. However, the traumatic emotional effect of leaving a job and the work family can happen in many, many other ways.

Retirement can cause similar results to being UnChosen. And retirees know that it is coming. They will still have emotional issues. There is an additional level of permanency to retirement that can and does affect the individual. We spend a large slice of our life at work and interacting with our peers, customers, and vendors. Leaving the workforce creates a social void that if not filled in some fashion can leave an individual in depression and in a constant state of unhappiness. There is also a great amount of time to be filled. If that person does not have hobbies, money to travel, or philanthropic endeavors to fill their time they are left to their thoughts and a state of not knowing what to do with all that

UnChosen

time.

Retirees will also deal with the component of *who* they are. The same question will be asked: "What do you do?" In the short term the retirement event is celebrated and the career revered. As time passes riding the celebration will subside and if the individual does not become active in some manner they will fall into a void of lost identity and self-worth. America is a culture of doers. *Doing something* is valued greatly. Other cultures are not as critical and judgmental. Some cultures value rest and leisure. In America, it just makes us feel guilty that we are not 'doing' something.

Some retirees will need validation of their existence and continue to ride the credibility of their old job and career telling the same old stories over and over again. Without something new in their lives, they become stagnant, and unfulfilled.

Those exiting the military after years of service can have a difficult time adjusting to the loss of their role, the military organization, and the people they were serving with. For the military there is an additional mental and psychological adjustment from the military and government way of operating to the commercial work place. Change of culture is an enormous burden.

Lastly, some people will UnChoose themselves. Whatever

the reason, doing this can cause the same impact on the individual as if the company had cancelled "The Social Contract." The only difference is they have separated themselves from that work family. Those that have UnChosen themselves are one step closer to owning their life, path, career, and destiny.

Those most affected by the UnChosen experience will be Baby Boomers and a good portion of the Generation X crowd. Later Gen X, Gen Y, and Millennials may not be as affected. As the work place has changed, so has the status quo and expectations for later generations. Millennials especially understand and *expect* to have many roles in many companies throughout their career. They have never known, and may never know the feeling or concept of "The Social Contract."

---

For more information and to share your story, visit
www.UnChosenbook.com